Call Sign Chopper

The Sequel

Chris Nott

Chris Nott

CALL SIGN CHOPPER-THE SEQUEL

Published by StoryUp Media 2023

First Edition

Paperback ISBN: 978-1-916826-10-6
Hardback ISBN: 978-1-916826-11-3
Ebook ISBN: 978-1-916826-12-0

Editor: Julian Moseley, JulianMoseley.com
Cover design & formatting: Liz Raguindin, LizRaguindin.com
Book and Publishing Consultant: Rob Culpepper, MrBookCoach.com

StoryUp Media
StoryUpMedia.com

Dedication

To my family, especially my wife Frances for her love and support

And Corwin Noble (RIP), my friend in adventure

Foreword

A Journey Beyond Imagination

It's with great honour that I invite you into the extraordinary world of Chris Nott. Our friendship has been a source of inspiration and camaraderie as we embarked on his second book and publishing journey.

For those of you who've had the pleasure of reading "Call Sign Chopper," you've already been introduced to Chris's life. A narrative that rivals the most thrilling espionage novels. The story begins with a 13-year-old boy, filled with dreams of becoming the iconic James Bond. The year was 1963, and it was "Doctor No" that ignited the spark of adventure within Chris.

But life has a way of unfolding in unexpected ways, and so it did for Chris. His early years were far from glamorous, leading him to clerical work at the Ministry of Defence, a world far removed from shaken martinis and sleek Aston Martins.

Yet, the beauty of Chris's story lies in his resilience and unwavering spirit. He transitioned from clerical work to the brave world of policing, dedicating 26 years to serving and protecting his community in Bristol, England. When a car accident curtailed his police career, Chris didn't let it deter him.

He embraced many new challenges.

It was during this time that his life took a unique turn. The BBC sought him out to star in their new documentary series, "Muscle," and Chris unexpectedly found himself in the limelight.

His journey took an astonishing twist when he was sent to Los Angeles to train as a weapons-carrying bodyguard. Impressed by his skills, an elite team of mercenaries, entrusted with guarding the president of Haiti, invited him to join their ranks.

From the streets of Bristol to the enigmatic world of Voodoo and mercenary work in Haiti, Chris's journey unfolds in ways that are both mesmerising and heart-pounding. His vivid descriptions of the violent revolution will transport you to a world you've never imagined.

As a friend, book coach, and publisher who's shared in Chris's incredible writing adventure, I can vouch for the fact that his first book, "Call Sign Chopper, is a testament to the incredible power of human spirit, ambition, and the unrelenting pursuit of dreams.

I'm honoured to introduce you to his much-anticipated second book, "Call Sign Chopper - The Sequel."

Brace yourself for the next chapter in Chris's extraordinary odyssey, filled with action, intrigue, and a spirit that shows dreams can transcend circumstances.

I'll end with a life-changing quote that rings in my ear every time I think of Chris and his adventures. It's a quote from Chris we should all strive to live by...

"Never Let Your Memories Become Greater Than Your Dreams"

Rob Culpepper
Book and Publishing Consultant
MrBookCoach.com
Barcelona, Spain
November 2023

Readers Note

I have attempted to use authentic Haitian Kreyol patois which is based on French with some Spanish flavouring. Interwoven is an influence of American English which pervades in the Caribbean and which may seem out of context at times.

Before the separation of the Island into Haiti and The Dominican Republic, it was known as Hispaniola. Therefore speech and place names may not translate exactly.

Additionally, spelling and pronunciation vary regionally much like English dialects the world over. Some words I spelt phonetically.

Other things are confusing as well, e.g. when talking about monetary values 'mill' = 100 not 1000 as one might expect.

So, please accept that if what you read makes only partial sense, remember an often-quoted expression, 'This is Haiti'.

Just like in my first book, the stories are all true. A few names have been changed to protect their privacy. I hope you enjoy.

Also Note:

Due to the devastating earthquakes in 2010, 2011 and 2023, in which more than 250,000 people perished; buildings, roads, locations and infrastructure disappeared.

Sadly, the people and places I refer to may no longer exist.

Chris Nott

CALL SIGN CHOPPER-THE SEQUEL

Table of Contents

Chris Nott

CALL SIGN CHOPPER-THE SEQUEL

Chapter 1
OUT OF AFRICA!

N ovember 2003. Back home in one piece after my incredible, adrenaline-infused Haiti adventure, I sulked for a few days then mentally drew a line under it.

What next? Back to working as a "bouncer" on the doors of nightclubs? After the heady, intoxicating, nerve-jangling excitement of Haiti, anything else would be a total anticlimax. The only prospect which offered a hint of overseas stimulation was the maritime security job which I had started doing back in 1996.

I decided to make a phone call to let them know that I was back home and available. The conversation went something like this:

"Oh yes, Chris! How are you?"

"I'm OK thanks, and keen to work, do you have anything for me?"

"Possibly, we still have some relief work on the US prepositioning fleet in the Med. You fancy that?"

"Yes, sounds good to me."

"OK, I'll get back to you."

"All right, thanks."

I didn't want them to think I was desperate, but the truth is, I was! Once you've experienced the kind of knife-edge existence that I had just left behind, you'll grasp at anything, even a pale imitation.

Once again the sea was calling. I got the callback and was able to complete a number of deployments on various ships of the prepositioning fleet, the longest in duration being 10 days. These were easy gigs, basically unarmed patrolling of the decks, shouting at any small craft that came too close to the vessel. This had been brought about by the attack on the USS Cole some years earlier. Although not the best paid of jobs, the off-duty time compensated for it, as we were generally berthed in some of the best ports around the Mediterranean Sea. I looked upon these jobs as paid cruises, and was settling into a routine of doing the odd bit of security work locally, then jetting off to the Med for short "paid cruises". I was coming to terms with the fact that my pulse wasn't going to race too often.

Towards the end of January 2004, I was offered a two-week job on a grain ship in Mombasa. Just the fact that it was in Kenya was enough to excite me! I was right up for it and felt that things were looking up, maybe. Bags packed, I was off to Africa for 10 days. It was easy work, just being on deck, busy monitoring the labour force that had been brought in to work on the grain discharge. We took charge of the labourers' identity cards, which they had to produce in order to work. There were two 12-hour shifts, but most of the labourers worked till they dropped, then slept on the deck for no more than three hours, after which they went back to work. The grain had been donated by the Catholic Church of America. A stream of open-backed trucks queued up on the dockside to be filled, after which they were lashed down, and then drove off.

This went on non-stop, 24 hours a day, day in, day out. It must have been day five when a member of the Catholic Church (the grain donor) came on board to watch the trucks fill up and drive off. I was on duty at the time and we had a conversation. As we watched the fully laden trucks drive off out of the port, we agreed that it was a good thing that they were doing. However, when I asked how they could be sure that the grain was going to the people who really needed it, his reply was, "I trust in the Lord". Being the cynic that I am, I found it difficult to stifle a snigger. I did ask if he had any way of checking on this but he emphasised his trust in the Lord. I didn't press him any further. By day seven, the grain silos were empty. Our final duty was to complete a stowaway search before the ship could leave port. That being done, we disembarked and made our way to the airport for our flight home.

Whilst we were queueing, an announcement was made:

"Would anyone be prepared to give up their seat to allow refugees to board? You will be compensated and put up in a hotel to await your next available flight."

As a team we were tempted by the idea of an extra day or two of rest and relaxation, so we went up to the airline desk. They offered to put us up in the White Sands Hotel – the best hotel in Mombasa, plus a cash allowance of 100USD per night! The team leader immediately phoned the office and told them that we had been bumped off the flight. The company then agreed to pay us our daily rate, too! So, "double bubble"! Off we went to the luxurious White Sands. Drinks all round! Two days of paid holiday. Sometimes the gods did smile down on us.

The evening of the second day we boarded our plane to Nairobi where we were to connect with our flight to London. After much delay in Nairobi we found ourselves in the queue waiting to board. I struck up a conversation with a couple who turned out to be veterinary surgeons with a practice in Nyali, north of Mombasa. They gave me their email address and invited me to visit the next time that I was in town.

Back home nothing much was happening. I was intrigued by the vets' invitation. Having now tasted Africa, I wanted more. I whizzed off an email to them. They advised me that they often took on volunteers to help out around the surgery and that they would arrange lodgings for me with a family in the local town, Mtwapa. In fact, the Med ships had lost their appeal since my African trip, so it wasn't long before I'd again packed my bags and was heading for Heathrow and a flight to Mombasa. I was greeted upon arrival by a male family member who then drove me to Mtwapa, where I met the rest of his family, which was two sisters, a couple of aunties and a whole flock of children! Later on I was picked up by the vets and given a guided tour of the area. It was agreed that I would be driven to the surgery each day, the cost of which would be included in the rent for my accommodation. Everything was settled. The routine was to spend the daytime hours with the vets and the evenings with the family, who liked to go to the beach, sit and drink hot, sweet, strong black coffee and chew khat (narcotic herb). They added chewing gum to the khat to take away the harsh bitter taste of the herb. The adult family members would be joined by various friends. They would all sit around chatting, sipping and chewing, watching the sun go down and the monkeys cavorting about the water's edge. The khat seemed to have a soporific effect on them. I tried it one evening but it did nothing for me, so after that I took Tusker beers with me instead.

Days and evenings came and went. Everyone was very kind and I was well looked after; However, I was disappointed that the vets only dealt with domestic animals. The evenings quickly bored me. One evening, for a change we went to the East Africa Safari Club. I met Dr. Zahoor Kashmiri there, otherwise known as the "Tarzan vet". He was well known from his wildlife television programs. We hit it off immediately and he suggested that there could be a job for me as his security man when he went into the bush to rescue animals that had been caught in poachers' traps. I had by now become more independent, using the local matatus (bus service) to get from Mtwapa to the vets. In the evenings I started to frequent the Nakumatt in Nyali, where there was a really good supermarket, restaurant and cyber café, where I could keep in contact with family and friends.

One evening I was with the family and friends at the East Africa Safari Club. The Tusker beer was refreshing me nicely when Zeinab, the elder sister, took a phone call. She burst into tears! It was her mother breaking the news of the death of her father. The parents had been separated for some time. He had been living in Jomvu, about an hour's drive from Mtwapa, where his neighbours had contacted the police, as he had not been seen for a few days. The police had broken into his house only to find him lying dead on his bed. Both sisters were now in floods of tears and wanted to go to him. I paid my condolences and they made arrangements to go to Nyali police station, but I was told that I was now family and that I must go with them. How could I refuse? After a tearful drive we were at the police station on Moyne Drive. The officers wore camouflage combat jackets, looking more like the military than regular cops. They were sympathetic and arrangements were made for the sisters to collect their father's body to convey him to the Coast Province General Hospital, where he would be kept until he could be buried the next day, in accordance with Muslim practice.

We had engaged a private ambulance to collect the body. I had ascertained from the cops that dad had probably been dead for at least a day and that there was no sign of any crime. He had been suffering from a heart condition for some time, and his death was not unexpected, therefore it had been agreed that the body could be released to the family for burial the following day. The sisters wanted me to accompany them to see their dad, as I used to be a cop and was used to these things. I warned them that since he had been dead for a while and in this heat, he wouldn't be a pretty sight. They were adamant that they wanted to see him. I had a sister on either side of me clutching my arms. As we walked up to the door, the officer who was standing guard at the front door checked the sisters' identity. I could hear the ominous buzzing sound. I again asked the girls if they really wanted to do this and that it would be better to remember dad as he was in life. They insisted on seeing him. The cop opened the door into the single-roomed dwelling. There was a swarm of flies buzzing around the grotesquely-swollen body. The sisters burst into floods of tears. I hugged them both and walked them away from the door as the ambulance crew went in to complete their gory task.

The next day I didn't attend the actual funeral as I'm not a Muslim but I was invited to the wake. The women were traditionally dressed in *buibui,* (black full length gown with head covering) appropriate for the occasion. They sat on one side of the open-air reception area and the men, dressed in Western, non-traditional clothing sat on the other. We were fed *ceema* (savoury dough) as a starter, then the woman who was in charge of the cooking went into the kitchen and some minutes later carried out a large tray of roasted goat. As she approached me, a swarm of flies descended onto the meat, immediately evoking visions of the previous evening. One of the men told me that I was a guest of honour and would receive first choice. She made a valiant effort of trying to swipe the flies away but with little success. She stood before me with the tray. Not wanting to cause any offence, I made a grateful show of accepting the offering and ate heartily, all the while worrying how my guts would react hours later!

That evening I reflected on my time in Kenya and concluded that I was getting in too deep. I went to the cyber café and opened an email from my mate Corwin. Corwin was a former US cop who I had met when I was working on my last Haiti deployment two years previously, as a member of the presidential protection unit, tasked with keeping President Aristide in power. He and I had instantly gelled. I had been curious about him as he was the only black man on the team. It was a standing joke that he was a "blan" (white man). As our friendship grew, he confided in me that he was working for the United States Drug Enforcement Agency (DEA) and that if anything went wrong he could blend in with the local populace and escape. Corwin introduced me to two of his contacts from the American embassy in Port au Prince. We had regular Sunday morning coffee meetings in the Villa Creole hotel. After he was deposed, Aristide fled to South Africa where he was last heard to be living in exile. United States law enforcement agencies had been investigating the former president for his involvement in shipping vast quantities of cocaine into the US.

Corwin was in Kurdistan, Northern Iraq and recruiting! That made my mind up that it was time to go; the money was right and it would be with some of my old Haiti crew, Ed and Martyn. My perfect reason to leave the family and move on. The next day my stomach was remarkably stable. I gave them the news. There were hugs all round. I took a matatu to the vets, and there were more hugs and good wishes. I then went to the Nakumatt cyber café and emailed Corwin, accepting his offer and telling him of my current whereabouts. I did of course phone home to discuss these developments with Frances. She was my rock, as ever. She gave me her backing, knowing that I had to do it.

Once again I was heading into unknown danger, but at least I felt her love and support. I had to go home first and sort things out, but the next available flight wasn't until the evening after, so I needed to find overnight accommodation. The Glory Villas was the right price and it had a swimming pool, but a more apt name would have been "The *Faded* Glory Villas"! The sign in the reception said it all really. "No prostitutes permitted in rooms" and "No khat"! It was a bit of a comedown from the White Sands of some months ago, but not the worst hotel that I had ever stayed in. I spent a pleasant morning by the pool before taking a taxi to the airport and boarding the plane for home and my next adventure.

Dr Zahoor Kashmiri

Following my departure from Kenya, Dr. Kashmiri and I maintained regular email contact, exchanging messages on average once a month or so. I would update him of my latest adventures and he would tell me about future business plans which he wanted me to be a part of. It was ironic that whenever I was back in Mombasa, he would be elsewhere in Africa rescuing injured animals from poachers' snares, so we unfortunately never got to meet again. The years passed by and after roughly five years my emails were no longer answered. I was initially a bit miffed but accepted that he had decided on a different course of action, one that didn't include me. It was late 2008 when I was back in Mombasa on a mixed cargo ship, engaged in rear loading ramp duty, when I struck up a conversation with one of the local dockside security men. We talked of life in general and specifically Kenyan life. I asked him about the "Tarzan Vet" television series. His reply hit me. I remember his words precisely: "Yes, I loved that programme. So sad, Doctor Kashmiri was killed by an elephant he was rescuing in Ethiopia, he is no more". RIP, Doctor Kashmiri.

Chapter 2
MY LAST NIGHT IN THE GLORY VILLAS

F resh out of the shower and changed, I was ready for my last night in Kenya. I appeared to be the only punter at the poolside bar. Sam the affable barman was keen to chat. He was interested in my reason for being in Kenya, so I told him the story. He was relieved that I wasn't a "do gooder" from the West, telling them how they should live their lives. He went on to tell me the following story.

Some years ago a group of missionaries had visited a local village. They were appalled that the women and young girls had to walk for miles to the river to do the laundry and collect water every day, carrying heavy plastic water containers balanced on top of their heads. The missionaries decided that they would build a well in the village, giving them instant flowing water. Everyone was delighted and the work was completed in no time. A ceremony was held to declare the well open. Hymns were sung and it was a joyous day as the locals saw the spigot being turned and the water flowing. The grateful villagers sang and danced to show their appreciation. The missionaries left the next day.

Three months later the missionaries revisited the village and were upset to find that the well was not being used. In fact the village headman had banned its use. The reason he gave was that the well had destroyed centuries of village culture. Perplexed, the missionaries wanted to know how on earth this could be. The headman explained that for as long as anyone can remember the women of the village had walked to the river each day, where they had spent their time doing their laundry, socialising, gossiping, laughing, singing and complaining about the men. Meanwhile the men would idly tend to their cattle and the small patch of crops that grew around their huts. At the same time they would smoke and drink their homebrewed alcohol whilst having a laugh and a joke with their mates. The women would return and be busy preparing food. That was the time-honoured way of village life. The well had meant that the women didn't leave the village and their chores were completed in quick time. They didn't socialise, gossip, sing or laugh together. Jobs done, the women returned to their huts. They had nothing to do so they joined the men in drinking. As a result, domestic violence had manifested itself. The village headman had called a summit and made a proclamation that they should return to the traditional ways in order to maintain village harmony. I reflected on this story, yet another example of the arrogant West telling others how they should live their lives.

Chapter 3

KURDISTAN, NORTHERN IRAQ

A fter returning from Kenya I took a couple of days to get my bearings. I reconnected with family and friends and gathered my thoughts. I had always promised myself that I would live my life in reverse. After a stable younger life, I sought an unstable older life. My mantra "Never let your memories become greater than your dreams" played in my psyche.

Kurdistan and Iraq, a post-war conflict zone? That'll do nicely!

Since the war and the fall of Saddam Hussein, Iraq had opened up to become a magnet for adventurers from around the world with the prospect of big paydays. That is, if you were able to survive! I talked it over with Frances. She was somewhat less than enthusiastic this time. I told her that I would be with good mates who we both knew were solid and that the rewards would help give us financial security. She knew me well and once more gave me her support and love. A few days later, with my affairs in order, I found myself once again at London Heathrow airport, waiting to board my flight to Amman, Jordan.

The flight to Amman was long and tiring. I lugged my backpack into the arrivals section where I saw a man in Arab attire holding a piece of A4 white paper with "Mr Chiris" scrawled on it. He greeted me with "Taxi". I was feeling quite weary as I clambered into his car and we sped off to the Grand Hyatt hotel. Upon checking in, the reception staff told me that my car would be there to pick me up in the morning. By the time I got to my room it was approaching midnight. I flopped onto the sumptuous, king-sized bed and I was out like a light in seconds. I was in the deepest of sleeps when an annoying "something" lifted my level of consciousness. It was the bloody bedside phone ringing! I reached out and scrabbled around to pick up the handset.

"Mr Chris, your car is here."

I managed a feeble "OK" as I saw the time on the digital clock, which told me that it was 2am! I felt dreadful! I dragged myself out of bed, forced a quick wash and a shave. The phone rang again.

"You are awake? You must come now."

"I'm coming, give me five minutes", I tersely replied.

Like most people I'm not good when my sleep is interrupted. Kit gathered together, I stumbled down to the front desk and handed in my card key. The receptionist told me that my car was outside. I emerged from the cool air conditioning and hit the warm night air. Right in front of me was an ancient Nissan Sunny with its engine running. The cigarette-smoking driver introduced himself as Faz and told me that if I was Mr Chris he would take me to Al Mansour, Baghdad. My heart sank. As a dedicated non-smoker, this was going to be an ordeal! I confirmed my identity, threw my backpack onto the rear seat, jumped in next to it and deliberately lowered the windows. There was no point in asking or telling him not to smoke, as my experience had been that Middle Eastern men considered it a manly habit. He told me that the dead of night was the safest time to travel.

Off we set at an insane speed. It was clear that Faz spoke little English. He told me that he was trusted and regularly did this route across the "empty quarter" to Baghdad. He opened the glove box to reveal an old revolver nestling amongst various cigarette packets. I felt so reassured! We raced out of Amman with the warm wind buffeting my face and we were in the desert in no time. As the sun rose the arid landscape slowly revealed itself. It was rocky, pinkish brown dirt, not the golden, gently-rippled sand and dunes which I had been expecting. Faz told me that the "empty quarter" was a "very bad place". We were on a good tarmac road with the lightest of traffic, doing about 80 miles per hour. I did wonder if the Sunny could sustain this pace. Faz told me that we should get there in around 10 hours or so. "Deep joy!" I thought, as I settled back into my seat. The journey was uneventful; we negotiated some military checkpoints and stopped a few times at roadside cafés for sweet milk less tea, served in small, narrow-bodied glasses. I didn't fancy any of the food I saw on offer.

Faz finally dropped me off at an anonymous villa in the district of Al Mansour, Baghdad in the early afternoon. A local man who was expecting me came to the door and showed me around the villa. There was a refrigerator with food and drink inside. I dumped my kit in a bedroom allocated to me for the night. I was told that a taxi would pick me up at 0800 hours to take me to the "green zone", the American-controlled area of the city, to be issued with my US Department of Defense permission to bear arms. He then left and I made myself at home. I watched a little BBC World News and had an early night. The next day, my taxi was there on the dot. Dil was my driver. We were surprisingly well received by the US Military, who controlled the "green zone". They seemed to be aware of me and what my mission was.

My passport was examined, identity photo taken, documents issued and I was off! Dil told me that it was a five-hour drive to Erbil in Kurdistan. Unusually, Dil was a non-smoker.

The miles were eaten up. As we drew close to Erbil there was obvious military activity. US troops were very much in evidence, along with the local Peshmerga militia. At around 1400 hours I was delivered to the "team house" which was situated in Ankawa, the Christian district of Erbil. It was protected by large, anti-ram concrete bollards and armed guards. I was met by Ed, who seemed pleased to see me. He gave me the in-country brief and a rundown on what-was-what. He finished off by telling me that we were in virtual lockdown, somewhat different from Haiti! There was at least a bar in the UN compound which could be reached on foot. He handed me my Russian-designed AK-47 (though I was told the ones we were using were Chinese manufactured) and my Taurus handgun. He advised me to get some sleep, since the procedure with all new team members like me was to have them perform night shift duty, in order to ease them in gently.

At 1800 hours, after a decent two-and-a-half-hour kip, I was in the control room with Chas, a former US Marine. He did his best to explain the technology to me. I'm a bit of a technophobe. He left me after about an hour, reasonably confident that if I heard or saw anything wrong I would know how to raise the alarm. In any case I could, if I wanted to, go out on foot and visit our local guards. As me and technology are not the best of friends, I did just that. I went out on foot patrol to make acquaintance with the guards. One or two spoke a little English. I ascertained that they, like me, worked 12-hour shifts. I returned to the control room, plugged my laptop into the power supply and clicked on a morale-boosting, "Carry On" movie (a hugely popular British iconic

1960's risqué comedy genre, still shown on TV today). Subsequent night shifts followed this pattern. Foot patrol, watch an 007 movie, foot patrol, watch a "Carry On" movie, and on it went until 0600 hours whilst, of course, monitoring the CCTV screen. I was now at night seven, my final night before a day off. So far no untoward incident, nothing to write in the log, apart from "on patrol" and "control".

It was about 0300 hours and James Bond had just vanquished a couple of arch villains. I was busy sipping a hot chocolate when I heard the distinctive sound of a "double tap" – two gunshots in quick succession. I checked the CCTV monitor where I could see our guards milling around. Immediately I'm moving tactically, my AK cocked and into my shoulder, ready to fire. Within seconds I am outside but under cover and in a good firing position. I can hear the sound of raucous laughter. What is going on? My personal radio crackles "Sitrep, sitrep?". It's Ed. Radios are set to "talk through", which means that each radio can monitor transmissions. I respond "Standby, standby, do not deploy, wait out". I continue to monitor the scene. In amongst the laughter I can make out a cry of pain. A 4-wheel drive vehicle reverses up to the guards. The rear door is open and I see a guard being bundled inside. The door is slammed shut and the vehicle speeds off. My brain is working overtime, I guess that some kind of incident or accident has occurred. I tactically advance. The guards turn towards me. With my finger on my radio prestel so that my colleagues can hear, I issue the friendly greeting, "salam alikum" (peace be with you). Amidst their laughter I hear the reply "wa alikum salam" (and unto you peace). That's a positive sign. They are not pointing their guns at me but are in fits of laughter, so I lower my weapon. One of the guards who speaks the best English approaches me and explains the cause of the commotion. I continue my radio broadcast as he describes how the bored guards decided to practise some military rifle drills. It all got a bit competitive and went beyond the basics! Apparently the injured guard had tried to twirl his weapon and a finger must have somehow slipped inside the finger guard and put pressure on the trigger. Stupidly, the safety catch must have been off, as he managed to "double tap" himself in his right foot! The comments and giggles that reached my ear from my radio were such that Ed had to call for radio silence. I got confirmation from the guard supervisor that the story was true. I confirmed to Ed that this was the case. Even so, I made a tactical return to the control room. My hot chocolate had cooled but was still drinkable.

The Coalition Provisional Authority, Erbil

The following day we were formed into a motorcade, much smaller than the presidential one in Haiti. As I'm sitting in the front right passenger seat, I notice a scattering of fine glass particles on the dashboard in front of me. Unthinkingly I pick up a chamois leather from the door pocket and wipe up the slivers. Red the driver chuckles.

"They didn't tell you?"

"Tell me what?"

"The last guy who sat there took one through the windshield", he said dryly.

"Nice", I murmured.

I was aware that the vehicles were used by other teams on other jobs. Was he testing my mettle? Was it a windup? No one had told me that we had recently lost a team member.

Off we set, our destination the Coalition Provisional Authority compound, Erbil. Once inside, our job was to bolster the armed Peshmerga militia. Our duties were straightforward guard duties, rotating fixed points throughout the day until it was time for the motorcade home. However there would be daytime excursions where we would escort USAID (United States America International Development. Government agency) representatives to visit projects which had applied for funding. Often these excursions would consist of myself, a driver and the representative, plus a briefcase containing 50,000USD! We would drive out into the desert to meet the local government official, who was usually flanked by armed guards in a single-storey building. The representative and I would approach him. We would be offered sweet, milkless tea. A few pleasantries would be exchanged, the cash would be handed over, and we would return to Erbil. Occasionally we would escort our clients into Erbil for business dinners.

I got into the habit of taking mid-morning tea at my post. I also like to dunk biscuits in my tea. I asked one of the "Pesh" (Peshmerga) if there were any shops nearby that sold biscuits. He said that there were, so I gave him a couple of dollars and asked him to get me some. Ten minutes later, he returned and handed me a clear cellophane pack with blue print on it, containing plain-looking biscuits. I thanked him. He kept the change without asking. I settled down on a low wall from where I had a clear view of my arc of fire. My tea was still hot. I went to peel the wrapper off the biscuits when I read the blue words printed on the packet: "World Food Programme". Puzzled, I looked closely at the pack.

It bore the distinctive logo of the United Nations World Food Programme.

I called the "Pesh" who had bought the biscuits for me. He confirmed that he had paid 1.50USD for them. He went on to tell me that the shop was full of UN food, all of which was for sale. I told him that this was food donated by the UN to distribute free to the starving poor people. He shrugged his shoulders and told me that I was a dumb Westerner. I challenged him over that comment. An involved conversation then ensued which became a little heated. Whilst we were debating one of my colleagues, Mikee, who was on roving patrol joined us and engaged in the debate. He was a "good ol' boy" from the Deep South, USA. The subject had somehow gravitated to democracy.

Mikee proclaimed, "But we have given you democracy, you can vote for who you want to govern you".

The "Pesh" looked genuinely perplexed. I will never forget his reply which was, "Why do I need to vote? I just want a strong 'father' to look after me and my family".

I asked myself there and then: "Who do we think we are?". The superior West poking their noses into the affairs of other countries and telling them how they should run their lives. Their ways may seem archaic, mediaeval and cruel to us, but who were we to tell them that they were wrong? How could it be right for us to impose our ways upon them, ways that we had evolved over centuries, ways that "we" were expecting them to accept without question? This conversation had a profound effect on me. It made me question my Western convictions of righteousness.

My four-month contract was coming to an end. They had given me the option to extend for another two years and I was considering it. But things had been happening at home; my wife Frances had sold our house and was living in a rented bungalow. She had paid a deposit on a new property that was under construction. I needed to be back home, not leaving her to deal with all the aggravation of moving house on her own.

Chris Nott

CALL SIGN CHOPPER-THE SEQUEL

Ankawa, Erbil, Kurdistan, Northern Iraq

21

CALL SIGN CHOPPER-THE SEQUEL

Tea Break Erbil, Kurdistan

Guard Duty Erbil, Kurdistan

Chapter 4
HEADING HOME FROM IRAQ

D river Sadar was given the unenviable task of delivering me to the Zhako border crossing and helping me get through the Iraqi side of officialdom. The journey was roughly three hours. The navigating of officialdom could range from less than one hour to whatever. Off we set, straight after breakfast. Sadar assured me that providing there was nothing to suggest that I had been working in Kurdistan, getting through customs and immigration would be a cinch, so long as I was happy to part with 100USD to smooth my way. When I was working in Haiti, a team member named Dick gave me some valuable advice: "Get yourself a fake Rolex watch. So that when you are in shit city and the last plane out is full, flash your "Rolex" to the loadmaster and get him to kick one of the nuns off in exchange for your watch. It's international currency!".

The opportunity arose for me to buy myself such a watch when I had been on a maritime security job in the port of Naples. A dockside hawker was selling his wares. I struck a deal and bought four fake Rolex watches for 100USD. I was wearing one of them on my left wrist as we approached the Zhako border crossing. We joined the queue of vehicles leading to the security checkpoint. I lost track of time as we sat waiting to clear the vehicle security checkpoint. Turkey was and still is at war with the Kurds, hence the tedious security formalities. Eventually I was safely through security. Sadar wished me good luck as he dropped me off at the immigration hall. He had briefed me that it would be chaotic and that it would be down to me to push my way through the crowd to the desk as there was no queue system. I entered the hall with my bulky backpack firmly strapped to my back.

The scene before me was utter chaos. I was the only Westerner in the hall. In fact the crowd seemed to be all adult males. There were no women or children to be seen. Men were pushing, shoving, jostling and shouting in order to get to the desk to get their documents checked. I stood back for a while to take in the scene, to see if there was any clue as to the best way to push through to the desk. I watched as a concerted crowd surge threatened to overwhelm the immigration desk. The three officers behind the desk rose up and started to beat back the oppressors with batons. Another officer appeared and stood up on the desk shouting and berating the unruly crowd. To emphasise his seriousness he drew his hand gun and held it aloft. This coupled with a number of split skulls pouring blood had the desired effect. The crowd calmed. I took this as my cue to forge my way from the back of the hall to the desk. I made good progress through the less enthusiastic back half of the crowd. It took my rugby-playing expertise gained as a young man to get me within two or three bodies of the desk. I managed to catch the eye of one of the officers and he beckoned me forward. I guess this must have upset those in front of me, as they turned and started lashing out at me. The blows were ineffectual. I returned a few good cracks to the jaws of my adversaries. One sank to the floor. This spurred others to turn on me. I was now through but I had my back to the desk and was fighting off my assailants. I was way outnumbered and it was only a matter of time before I would be overwhelmed. I was firing blows out, concentrating on those immediately assaulting me.

I was getting tired and some of their blows were getting through. I became aware of batons raining down on the heads in front of me. The crowd was pulling back. I quickly looked left and right. I saw that an immigration officer was either side of me standing on the desk and they were beating off my attackers. I felt a hand on my shoulder and heard the word, "passport" from behind me. I turned and fished my passport from a zipped pocket of my safari vest and handed it over. I heard the thump of his stamp as he asked for my "exit fee" of 50USD. I handed the cash over and he indicated that I should move to customs to check my backpack. I pushed my way towards the relative calm of the customs desk. I was breathing heavily as I unstrapped my pack, laid it on the desk and unzipped it. The official asked me what the contents were and I told him. He requested that I empty my bag. I held it open with my right hand and started pulling out my clothes with my left hand and placing each item on the desk. He is asking me about Kurdistan, I tell him that I have been working in an office in Baghdad.

As I'm talking to him I notice that his eyes are following my left hand. Once all my belongings are out of the pack and on the desk on display I deliberately rest both my hands palms down on my backpack. His eyes are fixed on my watch. He looks at me and points to the watch then makes a "give me" gesture with the fingers of his upturned hand. I make a resigned exhalation of breath sound as I unfasten the fake Rolex and hand it to him.

"Go!" he orders.

I gather up my kit and stuff it into my bag. I'm off out of there. Emerging from the hall, I instantly spot my next driver with his white card bearing my name, "Mr Chiris". I didn't hang around and made my way to the car. I threw my pack onto the back seat but before I got in I took a look in the wing mirror to check out my fat lip and swollen right cheek. My knuckles are bloodied and the front of my polo shirt is blood spattered. Goodbye Kurdistan, I'm heading home.

Chapter 5
THAILAND AND BACK TO HAITI

It was early summer, I was back home in England and settled into our temporary accommodation, a nice rented bungalow. Our new home would not be ready for us to move into until August. As usual it wasn't long before I was looking for my next job. The previous year had seen the advent of the Security Industry Authority, which was a national vetting and licensing scheme for those who worked in a security role in bars, clubs, licensed festivals or events. I applied for my licence in time for the music festival season and was able to work at the Glastonbury, WOMAD (World of Music and Dance) and Reading festivals, as well as having the odd three or four-day maritime job on ARC ships (American Roll-on-Roll-off Carriers), which plied their trade between either Zeebrugge or Bremerhaven and Southampton. All of which was for sure a far cry from the nerve-jangling, armed operations in Haiti and Iraq.

It was September when I saw an eye-catching advertisement in the National Association of Retired Police Officers (NARPO) quarterly magazine. It was for retired police officers to work on a "call out" basis for a worldwide disaster management company. Straight away I was on the phone to them. My telephone interview went well and I was subsequently enrolled on their two-day induction course the following week. The course was a brief introduction to the scope of their role, which was mainly one of dealing with the aftermath of air crashes. The course members were a lot like me; crusty, old former cops or medical types with whom I shared a similar dark humour. To counter that, there was also a smattering of young archaeology students, but believe it or not, we all got on well. It felt good to be with a bunch of like-minded people. At the completion of the course we went on our separate ways to various parts of the UK. I was really keen to get involved in this kind of humanitarian work. However, due to the nature of the business, for this to work out it obviously meant that something bad had to happen somewhere. The weeks went by. Each night I watched the news with conflicting feelings of guilt and hope. I felt guilty about hoping something awful would happen. In any case, nothing happened.

Christmas Day 2004 was a happy family affair for us, but on Boxing Day that year the television news brought the horror of the Indian Ocean tsunami into vivid view on our screens. This was more like it! By the 3rd of January, 2005 I was already deployed, working in the company warehouse, packing crates of supplies for mortuary operations which were destined for Khao lak, Thailand.

After a month of logistics work I finally got my wish and I was on my way to Khao lak. The company had set up base in the Marriott hotel right on the beach and a temporary field mortuary had been built a few miles away. The team was made up of British and Americans - American Morticians and British Undertakers (basically the same thing), together with embalmers and general assistants such as myself. Our job was processing the bodies of Europeans that had been recovered and preparing them for repatriation. We were part of a huge international response in which British, European and Scandinavian police were involved and who were engaged in disaster victim identification. It was grisly work, but worthwhile and satisfying. It was a case of working hard and playing hard. As soon as work was done, we would head to the bar for happy hour. There was nothing like a few cold Singha beers to wash away the grim work of the day, followed by dinner, then a good night's sleep before facing the horrors of the next day. We did have some down time and as a group we visited James Bond Island, so called after the film *"The Man with the Golden Gun"*, as it featured heavily in that movie. I reflected back to my teen obsession with the 007 stories. At last I could walk in the footsteps of James Bond!

Our month's deployment came to an end and we returned to the UK. Home once again, my spirits slumped. I guess that it was like a form of post-event depression. Having been involved in something so momentous, then going back to everyday tedium and normality. But life carried on. There were more ARC ship jobs to Northern Europe and back to Southampton. The months were slipping by. I received an email from Corwin. He had left Iraq and had taken a supervisory security job with a telecommunication company in Haiti. He assured me that as soon as a vacancy arose, he wanted me out there with him. I had to talk to my wife Frances again. I put the proposition to her.

"How long is it this time?", she enquired.

"I'm not sure, nothing definite yet", I replied.

However we both knew that I would go if I got the call. The call came in the form of an email from Corwin in early October. I was a victim of the Vodou enticing me back.

Chapter 6
RETURN TO VODOU LAND!

W hen I had my initial brief for my contract I was informed that this was a "security detail", which encompassed all aspects of security, plus whatever else was considered appropriate. Basically we are armed taxi drivers for our multinational clients, who range from corporate executives to technicians and riggers. Our job is to escort them to sites and offices and provide protection. A bit difficult when a rigger has climbed 200ft up a pylon! We have 33 clients in the country at any time so we are quite a hectic taxi service. We also take them to restaurants for evening meals and later to bars.

Little did I know…

I've only been in the country for five days, but it feels like I never left. The job is great. We are in charge of security for the technicians and executives of a company which is installing a new telephone system throughout the country. This means our job entails, on a daily basis, escorting staff to and from the three office locations that they operate from. It also involves visiting installations and pylons which are situated around Port-au-Prince and Pétion-Ville. Some of the sites are located in remote areas that are held by rebels, and these require visits from time to time to check if they are still standing, or to see if they are in need of maintenance work. These trips are more like expeditions into jungle areas.

I'd been apprehensive about coming back, due to the fact that my last job involved protecting the president, who ended up being deposed following the coup d'état. The government I had previously been working for was now the opposition, which meant that the politically-attached street gangs who had carried out the slaughter during the uprising were now the "good guys". They had vowed to exact revenge on all former oppressors, and most of all "Aristide's blans" (that was us, his white security).

My first realisation that this was a different "ball game" was on landing at Toussaint Louverture airport in Haiti. Previously I would have been whisked in through VIP diplomatic channels, sipping coffee whilst my bags were recovered for me. Not this time! I was definitely in "steerage class". Immigration found something wrong with my entry form and sent me back to rewrite it! I then had to wait by the baggage claim for over an hour before collecting my case. I was picked up by Corwin. Then it was out into the madness of Haiti! The road outside the airport was teeming as usual, with people bustling between cars, donkeys braying and tap taps (open-back pickup truck taxis) everywhere, honking like crazy. A riot of colour, exhaust fumes, and the distinctive third world smell (a mix of rotting vegetation, garbage, animal and human excrement!).

We got into the Hyundai Terracan four-wheel drive and shot out into the fray of traffic, passing the UN sangars manned by Brazilian troops, past overturned burnt out cars, mounds of garbage and groups of chimères (politically-aligned armed street gangs). On my way for induction? The adventure had begun!

Chapter 7
HAITI PART TWO!

I've only been back for a week but I am already faced with the usual problems. In my apartment the sink is blocked, the toilet won't flush, the TV won't work and the internet connection is down. The power and water supply are irregular and on top of all that I have the shits, the same as everybody else!

Corwin had taken me to the Montana Hotel (unofficially the best in Haiti, no star system exists here). We had lunch there and he briefed me on the job, after which we went to the office. Whilst I was there, casually hanging around waiting to be seen by "Big Al" the boss, I happened to glance at the noticeboard where I saw four cards pinned up, like thank-you cards. Being nosey I took a look. They were in fact "thank you for rescuing me from my kidnappers" cards! In the last three months, four staff or spouses of staff had been kidnapped and recovered! More about the local "cottage industry" later. I was issued with my handgun, a CZ 9mm (Czech Republican) - we only take long guns on certain jobs. I picked up my car, a Hyundai four-wheel drive Terracan, and after my welcome chat we were off to my new home at Juvenat. I was positioned behind Corwin to follow him out of the compound into the traffic.

What you have to know about driving in Haiti is that there are no rules. No laws. If you want to drive on the left you can, although common consensus is to keep to the right. Also the roads are made up ad hoc. For example, what if some construction work is going on and there is excess concrete left over? It is just shovelled onto the road! Makes sense, doesn't it? There is no highway authority or coordinated road building. If you can afford it, you make up the road outside your home, if not, then it remains a dirt track. Consequently there are potholes and dirt tracks, even in the centre of town. It's a real life "Wacky Races".

I was amazed to see that Pétion-Ville now has a single traffic light, which is American style and is suspended on wires over the centre of the intersection at the Tiger Market on Rue Lambert. No one takes much notice of it though! I lurched forward into the "race", hard on Corwin's tail not wanting to get lost. Horns honking, tatty old trucks, tap taps, people and various kinds of animals such as goats, dogs and chickens, all in one big turmoil! It was like being asleep and having a bucket of ice water thrown over you. The easiest way to die in Haiti was due to the anarchic roads. Talk about getting switched on! It was electrifying survival driving.

I got settled into my place then it was time for dinner. I was taken to a new restaurant called Bucan du Gregoire. I couldn't believe it! It was like coming home. Lots of people there that I knew from my previous deployment, plus bar staff, waitresses and various local faces. There is a huge UN presence now, nearly every other vehicle is white with "UN" stamped all over it, ranging from sedan cars to tanks and armoured personnel carriers. UN check points are at all critical points. Similar to Baghdad in Iraq, the UN has set up a "green and red zone" system, and you really don't want to go into the red zone. Unfortunately some of our installations and offices are inside the red zone! When I arrived it was raining and apparently had been for a couple of days, which is only to be expected since it is the hurricane/rainy season. But today is different; the sun is shining, I'm in the Caribbean, getting paid, and having fun!

Our evening work load has thankfully been reduced due to an unfortunate incident with a client in a house of ill repute. The company subsequently issued a memo that forbade us from taking clients to brothels! We also provide heavily-armed escorts for high-value loads from the airport, such as SIM cards, cell phones and cash. One of our more interesting tasks though is independent hostage rescue. That means no police involvement (because the PNH, Police Nationale d'Haiti are the main culprits!). We also negotiate hostage returns (paying the kidnappers ransom and ensuring safe hostage recovery).

Last Friday night was the company's Gala Event at the New Hotel Karibe in Juvenat. Dinner, dancing, light shows, speeches, and 500 free cell phones! Anyone who was anyone in Haitian society was invited, from the de facto president down. The American ambassador, the bourgeois and the glitterati. It is a fact that the highest number of millionaires in the Caribbean are in Haiti, along with the highest number of desperately poor. The evening would not have looked out of place in the US or UK. Everything was going fine until it was time to issue the free cell phones! It is something that must be built into the Haitian psyche; if something is free then chaos follows.

By now people are drunk on the free-flowing booze. I was put on the door and had to eject drunks! This took me back a year or two! Other team members were protecting the girls issuing the phones. Then the distribution point for the phones was located by the crowd and we had to form a protective cordon around it. All good fun, no serious incidents, just amazing to see expensively-dressed men and women drunkenly brawling for a free $200 phone when they have millions. After all, each attendee had already received a free phone, so they were just after extras!

Chapter 8

ON THE JOB!

N ev, another Haitian-American team member and I were detailed to the store in Martissant, in Kafou. The store is set back from the main road and is at odds with the rest of the area in that a Westerner would easily recognize it as a cellphone store. Our job was to control access, prevent staff intimidation, and repel any gang attempt to take over the store. We were assisted in this task by four contracted security guards, who were armed with short-barrelled shotguns and .38 revolver handguns.

It had been a brisk day at Martissant, with a steady flow of customers but not many buying, just there for the give-away promotional gifts. It was coming up to 1500 hours when one of the guards who was operating the front door summoned me over because he'd noticed that a local gang member called Davinroy and his entourage were approaching. The guard had locked the door as a precaution. The glass was darkened, so we could see out but those outside could not see in. This little mob looked like they were straight out of an MTV hip hop video, all dressed in rapper style and "blinged up" with gold jewellery. The handguns they were carrying were obvious under their loose basketball vests. Our guard went outside to parlay. Lots of hand waving and raised voices ensued. Nev went out to take over. I moved to the open door where Davinroy could see me. He was refusing to be searched, but if he wanted to come in, he really had no choice.

After spotting me, I could make out that he was saying something about "blan là". Nev came back inside together with the store manager and we conferred. It turned out that Davinroy was prepared to hand his gun over to "blan là" (the white man), in other words me! His men would remain outside and be no trouble as long as I escorted him around the store. The store manager considered this a good move, as Davinroy had some status in the community, so if he bought a phone, it would promote business.

So, after much elaborate hand shaking and mutual admiration I took charge of his .38 revolver. Davinroy and I were shown around the store by Evilyna, the manager. From what I could ascertain he said he would think about it; he was offered substantial discounts but what he really wanted was a gift! We went back outside where I handed him his gun back. He wanted all this to be done very publicly; we went through the handshake routine again as we parted. Davinroy said to me "ou mwem zammi, bye bye" (you are my friend, bye bye). That was it, the gang ambled off, gabbling away. Honour intact. The store closed as usual at 1600 hours.

The weather is deteriorating today. Everyone is taking shelter and reports say it will get worse.

Chapter 9

IT'S POURING!

Tropical storm Alpha is centred over us. I'm getting ready to go to work when I get stood down. An assessment is made that few people will turn out to the stores due to the weather. My stomach and intestines, aided by a dose of Vermox 500, after battling with the invading bacteria and parasites have finally agreed on a truce. The sudden explosions have ceased. My internal warning systems are back in place so no more surprises, hopefully! Outside, locals are taking advantage of the rain; stripping off and taking "natural showers" or doing laundry. There will surely be fatalities, shanties will be washed away and bodies will stack up at the confluence of the open sewers in downtown Port-au-Prince.

If Haiti is the poorest nation in the western hemisphere, then Kafou, which includes the slum of Martissant, has to be one of the most impoverished areas. It is a steaming, stinking, cesspit on the edge of Port-au-Prince. Needless to say it's in the "red" zone. Being the power base for the chimères, the local politically-inclined street gangs who control the area, shootouts with Lavalas gangs are a daily feature of life there. The company has had a week of events promoting their new GSM system and are expecting huge crowds at their stores.

Chapter 10
LET'S GET THE HELL OUTTA HERE

O ur clients were not happy. They were mainly Bolivians, Ecuadorian or Slovenians and all had experienced their share of political discord. They were genuinely scared and they wanted out!

The company had agreed to fly them to the Democratic Republic, where they would be put up in a hotel until the political climate in Haiti had returned to its normal state of kidnapping, murder and mayhem! So, on Wednesday morning we gathered up our flock of terrified clients in the parking area outside the Villa Creole, where we formed a motorcade. An "advance" consisting of Bob and Pierre (both Haitian) set off; they were to open up the route for us. The motorcade was about a minute behind them and we were bound for the airport. Tad, Ali and I were the C.A.T. (Counter Ambush Team) and we were about a minute behind the motorcade. We headed through Pétion-Ville, the advance relaying information about the manifestations that were going on. Most of the burning barricades were now just smouldering, having burnt out overnight, so we were able to just drive through them. The locals manning the barricades were just lolling around, weapons at their sides. They had probably been up all night, and made little effort to stop us, so our six-vehicle motorcade bulldozed its way to the airport without incident.

CALL SIGN CHOPPER-THE SEQUEL

The scenes that greeted us outside the airport were reminiscent of the Americans leaving Saigon at the end of the Vietnam war. The place was under siege by hordes of people, all with the same intent, which was to get out! They were waving passports and trying to get on any plane going anywhere out of the country. Our motorcade forced its way through the throng. The company had booked their flights and the tickets were ready to be picked up. We formed a cordon and pushed our way through the crowd. Our clients debussed (controlled exit of bus passengers) and we hustled them through to the departure gate.

Job done! We returned to our houses and "lockdown".

So our lucky clients would be treated to a nice, all-inclusive holiday in the Dominican Republic, while we would be confined to our homes, and fast running out of rations! I'd got it wrong yet again!

Chapter 11
IT'S ALL BACK ON, INCLUDING THE RETURN OF BASHAR!

Lockdown had been lifted and our clients had returned from their sojourn in the "Dom Rep". However it has been a lively few weeks! Hostilities have resumed. The UN troops are in daily contact with the chimères. Rue Toussaint Louverture (Airport Road) is the daily shooting practice range once again! The body count is mounting. Last week UN intelligence reported that after a shootout, Airport Road was littered with bodies too numerous to count. Kidnappings have escalated.

Arnie and I had just flown in after completing our leave period when our plane was stuck on the tarmac. The reason given was that there was an intense tropical storm and the airport officials considered it too dangerous for us to deplane. So, there we were sitting, me in first class (I had accumulated enough American Airlines points to get an automatic upgrade) and Arnie with the "rabble", when my headphone music of New Orleans blues was interrupted by an outbreak of Christian hymns from the rear of the plane!

Arnie related the story to me afterwards. We had suffered a bumpy landing due to the weather conditions. Pastor John stood up, praised the Lord for delivering us safely and went on to regale the passengers with how he and his mission had come to deliver Haiti and the Haitians from evil. He'd asked the passengers to raise their right hands if they had found the Lord. Virtually everyone had, except Arnie! After two hours of being stuck on board we were eventually allowed off, with Pastor John blessing every one as they passed by him.

Three days later we were on duty when a radio message came over the air, bringing news of the latest kidnapping. Do I need to say any more? Pastor John and 12 of his mission had been snatched from the streets! To date they have not been recovered. There was also the German aid worker who got out of the airport and flagged down what he thought was a taxi (there is no organised taxi service here). He was promptly taken straight to Cité Soleil, the HQ for all kidnappers. He was ultimately returned minus his little fingers after a ransom of 3,000USD was paid by his employers.

Kidnapping is ingrained into the Haitian mentality and exists at every level. Every day an elderly woman who lives on the street sits at the corner of Rue Pinchinat and Rue Gregoire. She has two scrawny dogs, the mangiest mutts you can imagine! Dan and I would regularly give her food leftovers for her and her mutts. Last week Madame Patricia, as we know her to be, was distressed. *Bashar* (one of her mutts) had been taken. She showed us a tatty note demanding the payment of 2,000 gourdes for its safe return.

Dan and I suspected that this could well be a scam to extract some cash from us. But she seemed genuinely upset and we are both a soft touch anyway. We stumped up the cash, about 50USD.

We left her cuddling *t' Pieton* (the other mutt). We rationalised that she was very poor anyway and needed the cash. Two days later, I saw Madame Patricia with *Bashar* and *t' Pieton* tied together on a length of string. She explained to me that she had "made the drop" and had been confronted by a masked youth wearing a baseball cap. She'd handed him the cash, he'd given her the dog, and off he'd run. I asked her if she had any idea who the dognapper was. She replied that although she hadn't been able to see his face, she'd known who he was because she'd recognised his bare feet! He lived near her on the same street.

On the subject of dogs, I came across an incident the other day, on Rue Lambert near the Tiger Market. A woman was beating her tethered dog with a length of electrical flex. I hate to see cruelty of any kind so I stopped the car, got out and shouted "Madam poukisa ou frappe chen ou?" (Lady, why do you hit your dog?).

She screamed back at me, "Chen masisi, coopee gason chen" (the dog is homosexual and has sex with other male dogs). I started to laugh and say that was no reason to beat it. She was hysterical and started lashing at it again. I went to intervene. By now there were a few bystanders. It was at the point when I grabbed her wrist that the bystanders advanced towards me and made it very clear that I should keep my "nen blan" (white nose) out of it. The dog was "masisi" and had to have it beaten out of it. Homosexuality in any form is not accepted here. I realised that I would have to retreat and leave the dog to its fate. As I drove off, a couple of rocks rained down on the roof of the car.

CALL SIGN CHOPPER-THE SEQUEL

It was about 2100 hours and I had just dropped off my last client of the night when, turning into Rue Chavannes, I saw a man lying face down in the road. As my headlights were on him, I could see that his skull had been smashed in and blood was running down the road. His body was fast oozing life and judging by all the twitching, I figured that he wasn't long for this world. I stopped and got out of the car. There was no one about, at least I didn't see anyone. I knew that there was nothing that I could do for him but I just wanted to let him know that he wasn't alone as he left this world. With that I heard voices advancing towards me in the darkness. I could make out words like "blan", "frappe", "mouri". I immediately ran back to my car and drove off because if I had interpreted what I had heard correctly then maybe they thought I was responsible. I sure wasn't going to hang around to find out!

Juan Chavez is a smooth, suave Latino with the looks to go with it. He is quite senior in the organisation. A few weeks ago he started having Kreyol lessons at 2100 hours each Sunday night. It had been my turn to take him to his Kreyol class the other Sunday. We approached the location, which was off Delmas 48 (not the best of areas). The only light came from the almost-full moon, set in a cloudless sky, together with the occasional glimmer from the few houses that had generators. We bumped along a track off Delmas 48, splashing through the sewage. Juan Chavez indicated the building with the second-floor apartment where he attended his lessons. I stopped outside the 10-foot-high wall and sounded the horn. The armed security guard let him inside. I could see a female form on the balcony of the apartment and there was a low, flickering light coming from within, probably from candles. I saw them embrace and do the kiss on both cheeks routine, which is the accepted greeting here. They both disappeared inside the apartment. I settled back into my car seat, lowering the back rest a few notches. With the air conditioning set on low, I allowed myself to relax and took in the view. An old woman was cooking over an open fire by the side of the track. Two young men were sitting in the shadows smoking, about 30 metres in front of me and to my right. I lowered the front windows as it was getting too cold. The smell of the fire, the cooking and the sewage mixed together to make up that distinctive Haitian night odour.

After about half an hour, an old Nissan trundled past me and turned to enter the house, just beyond the apartment where Juan Chavez was receiving his lesson. The car stopped and the driver sounded his horn for the guard to open up. I could see that there was just the Haitian male driver in the car. I saw the two men come out of the shadows and casually walk the fifteen metres or so up to the Nissan. I saw them level their right hands. I saw the revolvers in their hands. I heard the explosion as they emptied their guns into the Nissan.

I immediately reversed about 20 metres and was around a corner and out of range. I jumped out of my vehicle, gun in hand, and hugged the wall. I took a peek around the corner and the Nissan was gone! So were the gunmen and the woman cooking. My cell phone goes off, it's Juan Chavez requesting immediate extraction. Well I think that's what he gabbled!

I pulled up outside the "Kreyol school". Juan Chavez came running out buttoning his shirt; well it was a warm night so he must have undone it because he got hot doing his studies! He jumped into the open rear passenger door. I slammed into reverse and we were out of there. After driving for a couple of minutes, Juan Chavez told me that both he and his "teacher" had witnessed the shooting. I couldn't quite work this out because normally a pupil faces the teacher. They must have been facing in the same direction, maybe part of some advanced teaching techniques? A check with UN intelligence revealed no reports of any shootings or murders in Delmas 48.

Chapter 12

KIDNAP ALLEY

A message came over the radio that during the previous hour, not one but two kidnapping incidents had taken place. One in Pétion-Ville—two American missionaries' teenage twin daughters had been snatched off the street by men in black wearing red headscarves, reminiscent of Duvalier's 1960's terror squads, the *Tonton Macoute*. The missionaries didn't see the need for security when God would protect them.

The other was on Route National 1—the airport road—known to the ex-pat community as "Kidnap Alley". This was the more "classic" one. The MO ("modus operandi" or "method of operation", in police terminology) being the PNH (Police Nationale d'Haiti) would stage a road check and ostensibly stop vehicles for routine checks. If they found a likely candidate then they would arrest them. However, the arrestee would not see the inside of a police station. Instead, the cops would interrogate their catch to assess their worth based on which agency was employing them, then make demands. This hostage was an expat employee of one of the many NGOs (Non Governmental Organisations) operating here. Again, their philosophy did not include security.

When the kidnap message came over the air, I was driving two Bolivian clients, both IT specialists around 25 years old, who had been working for the company for the past two months. Since they had been in the country they had not ventured outside of their hotel, apart from being picked up and taken to and from work.

They had both told me (in perfect English) how terrified they had been and how glad they were for me to be taking them to the airport; however, the Bolivians had heard the message and knew the route that we had to take! This did nothing for their confidence. They pleaded with me to just get them to the airport! As I entered Nazon in the "red zone", heading fast onto Route National One, I received a cell phone call from the Detail Leader and his basic message was, "It's your call ... blast through if you have to!". The Bolivians looked gripped with fear but insisted that they had to get to the airport. We are now on "Kidnap Alley", approaching Pont Rouge where the UN usually has a checkpoint.

Today, ominously no UN. In the distance I can see the PNH, four sitting in the back of a large pick-up truck with the rear end at right angles to the road (positioned for a reverse ram). Two PNH were positioned in the road, waving cars through. Traffic was moderate and was slowing to squeeze through the checkpoint. No way to blast through and no other way to get around. To my left there was a raised central reservation, too high even for my four-wheel drive. To the right the PNH pick-up was blocking my exit and I was in a single line of traffic, therefore reversing was not an option either. As I drew closer I told my Bolivians to duck down. They readily complied! One of the cops was standing in the back of the pick-up, his rifle in his left hand and shouting and signalling to the cops in the road. They had spotted my white face! A blan, so worth a check. I am three cars away.

By now I have my CZ9mm in my right hand, "one up the spout" and at waist height under the dashboard level. I am now in second gear with the front side windows down. The road cops are ambling in my direction and waving their left hands at me. In their right hands are their rifles. The cop standing in the back of the pick-up appears to be in charge and is giving orders.

Is this a genuine PNH check or is it a kidnap? If genuine, why had they not stopped any cars before me? Decision time! I am slowing to a halt almost level with the pick-up. I raise my gun and point it directly at the standing cop in the back of the pick-up. I say in a loud firm voice to the cops approaching me "Fe bak amba u zam" (move away, lower your guns).

They slowly comply.

The cop in the pick-up lowers his weapon. I keep my gun trained on him as I pass by he appears to be laughing. I hear him shout out "Pa gen pwoblém blan!" (no trouble white man). The two in the road step back and allow me to pass. I twist around in my seat, keeping my gun on the cop as long as I can as there's no way to accelerate due to the line of traffic.

As the road ahead cleared, I holstered my gun and sped away. I watched the cops in my rear view mirror. They made no attempt to pursue me. My Bolivians took a bit of persuading to sit up, but by now we were nearing the airport.

As I dropped them off they shook hands and hugged me! I now had to make the return journey back past the PNH check point, but on the other side of the road. Yes, I could have taken a different route to avoid them, but once you have made a point, it needs reinforcing! As I passed by I made a point of waving to the cops. They wave back in a friendly manner.

I reflect on the incident. What I believe happened was the cops had been "fishing". If I had been unarmed or compliant then they would have taken advantage, either robbed or taken us hostage.

They are philosophical; if they meet with no resistance, they take advantage. If it looks too difficult, then don't bother. It's business to them, no hard feelings!

Two hours later a report came over the radio: "Heavy gun fire, sustained fighting, UN under attack from chimères at Pont Rouge".

Chapter 13
HAITIANS HAVE SHORT MEMORIES

I can't believe that I have been here for one month already!

My initial fear that I would be a marked man from my last job here appears to be unfounded. I have run into people who would have gladly killed me when I was president Aristide's security. As a longtime Haitian observer pointed out to me, "Haitians have short memories. You are just a whore doing it for money? Pa gen pwoblèm!" (no problem).

It was about 0200 hours when I had just dropped off a client. I needed some milk for the morning so I called into the Tiger Market. The Tiger Market is an all-night gas station and bar hangout for off-duty cops, prostitutes and creatures of the night. It was bustling. I picked up my milk and joined the queue to pay. I was the only blan in the bar. Practising my observational skills, I became aware of a big man staring at me. He was at least 6 feet 6 inches tall and built like a UN tank! I let my eyes roll over him and continued to scan. As my gaze swept back to "UN tank", our eyes met! He started slowly moving towards me. When he was about 10 feet away he pointed his finger at me and snarled in a gravelly voice "Palais National?" I swallowed hard and responded, "Oui, pwoblèm pour ou?". With that he is now within arm's length.

A big smile breaks out on his face and as we shake hands in the elaborate Haitian manner he bear hugs me. All the time he is chanting "CAT, CAT, CAT. Ou retune, mw zammi blan". By now the whole bar area is aware and watching. "CAT" was the president's "Counter Attack Team". He had remembered me from when we had worked on presidential motorcades. The people in the bar were cheering and clapping! All was well! Huge sigh of relief! The CAT man still had his job and worked for Boniface, the new interim president. He explained to me that only the top people had been killed or escaped. Further down the ladder, the troops had simply switched allegiance.

Pétion-Ville looks in worse shape than when I left two years ago, as if that could be possible! The roads are worse, the rubbish is piled 10 feet high and open sewers flood the streets. There are noticeably more amputees, street urchins, packs of dogs and huge rats on the streets. The reason for the amputees and urchins was the killing and mutilation orgy of the chimère machete gangs that raged following Aristide's departure. No one can explain the increase in the number of dogs and rats. Another sad sight on the corner of Rue Panamericaine by Le Ritz is the Clinic Bon Santé, Petite Cuer, where every morning a group of women with babies assemble. The consequences of the rapes that also sadly took place during those weeks of turmoil.

Late one night, after dropping a client, I took a wrong turn and ended up in downtown Port-au-Prince. I used to go there regularly before to the Hotel Oloffson. for "Ram" Vodou rock nights. It was sinister; no street lights, rubbish stacked 20 feet high and towering above me, fires burning, streams of effluent, deserted except for shadowy gangs, sounds of gunfire, Vodou drumming. Just like a scene from an apocalyptic movie. No place for a "blan", so I got out of there fast!

I have had to do the "Kidnap Alley" run a few times since. The cops just wave me straight through. The Martissant store was shot up two days after I was there. Davinroy never got his free phone! I had two RTA's (Road Traffic Accidents), both non-injury, and two incidents of damage to my vehicle, caused just by negotiating the terrain!

Along with Hepatitis C, AIDS, and "bad guts" we now have to contend with a killer strain of malaria which has arrived from South America. Twelve cases in the last week, all expats, resulting in two dead and one in a coma! We are all on chloroquine. Apart from that, I am in the Caribbean, the sun is shining and I am getting paid!

Chapter 14
MEN OF GOOD INTENT

I t was early evening. I was in my room and just about to get into the shower. My phone rings, it's Corwin.

"Whatcha doin' this evening?"

"Washing my hair", I replied.

This had been a point of banter between us, as although I kept mine tightly cropped, he shaved his to his skull every other day.

"Be at the Bucan by 2000 hours, there's some guys I'd like you to meet."

"Ok, see ya there", I replied, intrigued.

From my previous time in Haiti I thought that I already knew all the characters worth knowing in Pétion-Ville, the "faces" who we referred to as the "usual suspects". I was 15 minutes early, ingrained in me from my previous police, military and security jobs, where there was always a handover period before each shift commenced. I strode into the bar, rolling my eyes over the punters, virtually all of whom I knew, if not personally then by sight. I was greeted warmly, smiling a nod of recognition, alternately shaking hands with those that I knew better. The female bar staff greeted me with the usual double-cheek kiss. Corwin was sitting at the bar. "You're late," he laughed. He, like me, had a background in police, military and security, except that his experience had been gained in the USA and mine in England. Notwithstanding that we both had the same timekeeping ethic. Corwin pushed the frosted glass of Prestige bière along the bar to me.

I sat next to him and said, "What's all this about then?".

"Chris, I just want to sound you out first."

"Sound away", I replied.

"My friends will be arriving dead on eight, we have time for you to decide if you're interested or not", said Corwin.

"You've really piqued my interest now, go on",

I encouraged. Corwin took a draught of his beer.

"I'm part of a group of local men of some standing in the community. We are not affiliated to any official organisation. Our intention is to do good wherever we can, from charitable donations to righting wrongs", he said.

"I'm not averse to helping good causes, but 'righting wrongs', what does that entail?", I enquired.

"That's where you and I come in", he said with a grin.

I'm getting an uneasy but excited feeling. I can't help myself. I was only too well aware of the disgusting actions of the kidnappers based in Cité Soleil. Two American twin teenage girls had been snatched off the street by men in black, wearing red headscarves. The girls' family didn't see the need for security when God would protect them.

The parents had paid the ransom for the girls. The twins had been returned, one dead and the other gang raped and traumatised. It was such a vile crime that it had even shocked some of the other kidnapping gangs.

"Corwin, I'm in mate", I said in a gruff voice.

A few minutes later I noticed three smartly-dressed mature Haitian men arriving and going to a side table. Corwin nodded acknowledgement to them.

"Thanks mate, I knew I could count on you."

Corwin had latched onto my use of the English word *"mate"* and had adopted it into his own vocabulary, but it sounded slightly incongruous in his American accent. We went over to join them. The introductions were business-like with firm handshakes. Jean, Nesly and Jineau. We sat down. Without being asked, Lovely the bar manager brought a tray of Barbancourt 5-star rhum, a jug of ice and 5 glasses. She made a fuss of us, administering the customary double-cheek kisses all round, in-between charging our glasses. Jean raised his glass and proposed a toast to the "men of good intent". We slugged our rhum. Corwin then addressed the group, telling them about me and my British police and military reserves background, our friendship and how we had had each other's backs on our previous Haitian adventure protecting the president, and during our Iraq deployment. They were mightily impressed with my unarmed policing in the UK. Jean appeared to be the leader.

"Down to business", he said. "We require training. From what Corwin has told me, together you have the experience and the skills to equip us to deal with a local problem."

Realisation was starting to dawn on me that these men were on a mission to crack down on the kidnappers, but just how hard did they want to crack down? Without any prompting they were unanimous that the recent kidnap of the girl twins was beyond the pale and that the only solution was for the perpetrators to be eliminated. At a previous "men of good intent" meeting it had been put to the vote. Without exception it had been agreed on and was now policy. Further discussions had taken place as to how this should be accomplished. Initially the thought was to hire mercenaries to do the job. However after more in-depth talks, it was agreed that this was a local Haitian matter that needed to be carried out by Haitians, and that it would enhance the profile of the "men of good intent" in the community. The three men before us were to be the main actors. Nesley spoke up and told us that equipment would not be a problem, as there were sufficient resources within the group to provide anything that we might need. Jineau spoke, addressing his colleagues.

"Gentlemen, shall we adjourn to the bar, and allow Corwin and Chris some time to discuss our proposition?"

The three men left us. I looked at Corwin, his face was set like black granite.

"Are you still in?", he enquired.

"Of course, you'll need looking after", I laughed. "We can help with intelligence, possibly some surveillance, then help them with training and their plan. Shame we won't be in at the kill", I quipped.

Corwin gripped my hand, looked me square in the eye, and gave me an imperceptible nod, which I returned. We rose from our seats and joined the others at the bar. Jineau handed us both a menu.

"Will you join us for dinner?" he asked.

We enjoyed a convivial dinner with general conversations. After-dinner cigars and brandy were brought to the table. I declined the cigar. Jean proclaimed "Back to business!". After an hour or so and feeling pleasantly intoxicated, it was agreed that we should go our separate ways, gather intelligence from our various sources and reconvene at the same time, same place one week later. The three men rose from the table together, shook our hands in turn, thanked us and left. Corwin and I felt it only right that we should finish off the brandy. We agreed that until we had sufficient intelligence we could not formulate a training programme or come up with a plan. The night was still youngish so we decided to start straight away. Corwin immediately got onto his phone, calling his official sources. I left and drove carefully to the bar St. Pierre where I spoke to my street contacts, parted with some *lajan* (money) and put the word about.

It didn't take long. There was a general revulsion at the kidnappers' actions over the twins. The next night I was accosted by one of the street *bouzin* (prostitutes). She gave me a name: "Beckham", and further told me that he was also responsible for mutilations and the cutting off of fingers and ears, along with other rapes and murders. Apparently the gang leader was a bit of a footballer ("soccer player", for my American readers). He worshipped the famous England star and had adopted his name. That was a start but we needed much more. Three nights later I met with Corwin and Jean in the bar St. Pierre. It transpired that the three of us had come up with the same "nickname"; furthermore he attended football training in Pétion-Ville at 6pm each Tuesday evening, after which he visited a local girl for post-training sex. We were getting there but still needed more.

Again I put some *lajan* in the hands of the street *bouzin*, asking for the name and address of Beckham's girlfriend. The next night I was sitting at the bar of the St. Pierre. I had just ordered my Prestige bière when a young woman approached me. She looked to be in her late teens but her face was drawn and she wore a sad, frightened expression. She was accompanied by Marie, one of the *bouzin* who I knew spoke some English. Marie introduced me to Jeslyn. I shook Jeslyn's hand. It was cold and she was trembling. Marie explained to me that Jeslyn was Beckham's Tuesday night girl and that he treated her badly. I bought drinks for them and we retreated to a table at the back of the bar, out of earshot of the few early evening drinkers. Marie told me that Beckham was a psychopath and that he enjoyed hurting women. My anger started to rise. It was obvious that Jeslyn was in total fear of him.

Through Marie I ascertained that Beckham came to her address each Tuesday night at 7pm, had violent sex with her, handed her a few *gourdes* (Haitian money) and left at 9pm. He then drove off like a maniac down Canapé Vert and on into Port-au-Prince. Marie slipped me a piece of paper which I put in my pocket. I told Marie to tell Jeslyn that her ordeal would soon be over. The girls finished their bières. Jeslyn looked intently into my eyes, took both my hands in her bony hands and squeezed hard. I felt the intensity of her stare. I felt emotional, my Kreyol escaped me and all I could think of saying was "bon chance" (good luck). She nodded, let go of my hands, turned and walked out. Marie walked with her, she turned her head and mouthed the words, "thank you". I retrieved the piece of paper from my pocket that Marie had given me. I read the address, downed my beer, walked purposefully to my car and drove off towards Canapé Vert. I found the address not far out of Pétion-Ville. I pulled over and phoned Corwin. Fifteen minutes later back in the St. Pierre, Corwin was sitting next to me with a Prestige in front of him. I gave him a rundown on the events of my evening. Corwin immediately phoned Jean and arranged a meet in the Bucan Du Gregoire bar the following night.

At 1945 hours the next night Corwin and I took our seats in the Bucan bar. The three "men of good intent" arrived together at exactly 2000 hours. We stood and shook hands. Drinks were ordered and Jean said his usual "Let's get down to business". We told them what we had found out, which added to their own knowledge of our man and his cruelty to women, his armed robbery, drug dealing and reign of terror in his local community. Jean told us that the three had conferred since our last meeting and that they had consulted with an *oughan* (vodou priest). The *oughan* had told them that the method of elimination must comply with Vodou ethos. In this way the stature of the oughan in partnership with the "men of good intent" would be reinforced amongst the good people of Cité Soleil.

"OK, so I guess you no longer need us?", Corwin asked.

"We need the insurance of your training, like shooting and driving tactics, in case things go wrong; we also need you to connect with Jeslyn", Jean replied.

Jineau waved the waitress over. She arrived at our table with an arm full of menus. Jineau said "You will join us for dinner?". Of course we would!

After a pleasant meal and interesting conversations about Haiti and the local community it was time for brandy and cigars. I sensed a pattern developing! Glasses charged, my offer to partake of a cigar declined.

"Down to business!", Jean declared. "We know what we want

to accomplish. What we need from you is shooting skills and some driving tactics should our plan go awry. Escape, evasion and self defence", he proclaimed.

"OK", said Corwin, "we can do that. Just to clarify, we are strictly training you in defensive tactics".

Jean nodded.

"Out of interest, would you like to tell us what your plan is, as you have obviously discussed it?"

Jean leaned forward, in fact we all did instinctively.

"Our plan is for the oughan to tell the good people of his parish that Beckham would very soon cease his reign of terror over them. His death would be sudden and violent and appear to be an accident. The oughan would visit Jeslyn at her room next Tuesday afternoon. He would perform a ceremony. He would give Jeslyn a potion to discreetly put into Beckham's drink. Beckham would then drive his vehicle in his usual reckless manner down Canapé Vert. About a mile or so down the road is a notorious right hand bend, where a number of vehicles have left the road and plunged down fifty feet into the ravine, to a certain death. In his narcotic state he would not be able to control his vehicle and his demise would be assured."

Jean and his conspirators sat back. Corwin looked at me, I looked at him. Corwin said it first.

"OK, but I can foresee potential problems. Firstly and most importantly is the danger to any other road users. Also what if the narcotic doesn't have the desired effects, he realises what's happened and goes back to kill Jeslyn?"

"We've considered that", said Jean, "then we would ram him off the road or shoot him dead. But an assassination is not what we want. This must be the result of a vodou punishment."

"OK", said Corwin, "let's meet Sunday and practise shooting and vehicle tactics".

The three men downed their drinks, stood up together, thanked us, shook our hands, turned and walked away.

Jean turned and said "I'll call you to make arrangements. Have a good evening, the check is open, I'll settle it".

Corwin and I eyed the half empty bottle of brandy and agreed that it would be rude not to! He called for more ice. We then discussed their plan and agreed that we should have oversight of the operation, hanging back in a counter attack role.

Training day was Sunday, and our three friends arrived plus two reserves, Bruno and Adz. We met in a lightly-wooded area on the Kenscoff road. We had selected this spot as it was away from any human habitation. In any case the only people likely to be in the vicinity would be subsistence farmers scraping a living from the land, who couldn't care less about what we were doing, and the sound of gunfire was not unusual or anything to get excited about. They brought their own .38 revolver handguns and ammunition, freshly purchased from the Pétion-Ville security shop. Corwin went through the fundamentals of marksmanship with them. We used some empty one-litre plastic drink bottles for short range target practice, which they all managed to hit. There was hardly any traffic on the Kenscoff road so we then went through some tactical driving and shooting drills. The "men of good intent" thrived on the training and were confident that if things went wrong that they could make their escape. At the completion of the day we adjourned to the Bucan bar for drinks and debriefing. Following a meal and more brandy we went our separate ways, agreeing to meet at 1900 hours on Tuesday evening.

On Tuesday evening at 1800 hours Corwin and I had finished our shift, grabbed a quick bite to eat and were heading up to Canapé Vert. We parked up on the edge of Pétion-Ville and made contact with Jean on his cell phone. We ascertained that all was going according to plan. The oughan had done his thing and the potion had been delivered. It was now time to just sit and wait.

The anxious minutes ticked by. Surveillance on Jeslyn's address reported a Haitian male entering at just after 1900 hours. The next report at around 1930 hours was that the male had left the premises in what looked like an agitated state, got into his Dodge car and had driven off at speed down Canapé Vert. Nesley set off in his car following him. After a few minutes Jean called to inform us that there had been a nasty accident on Canapé Vert. Things had happened too fast.

"Let's check Jeslyn, somethings wrong, he doesn't leave till nine."

Corwin and I get to Jeslyn's home in a few minutes. The door is open. I rush in and find her unconscious on the dirt floor. Her face is a bloody mess. I don't move her, and note that she is still breathing. Her right eyebrow is an open wound and bleeding profusely. Corwin knew what to do. He had already rushed back out to his car and returned within seconds, opening a military field dressing as he ran. As I am applying the dressing Jeslyn starts to come round. Corwin's cell phone rings and he answers it.

I hear him saying "OK, that's good, but Jeslyn needs to go to hospital, can you return to her address now?".

Jeslyn is crying and gripping my arm as she tells me that Beckham "frappé" (punched) her.

Adz arrives while Jeslyn is regaining consciousness and her composure. Adz translates what has happened. Jeslyn had been very nervous and Beckham had sensed her agitation. He suspected that something was wrong. He grabbed her, searched her and found the small brown bottle containing the potion in the front pocket of her jeans. He recognised that it was vodou. He flew into a rage, kicked and punched her unconscious. Adz pointed out to me the broken brown bottle on the floor and liquid contents splattered on the wall above.

"Can you take her to the hospital, Adz?", I ask.

"Certainly", he replies. Adz and I help Jeslyn into his car and off they go to hospital. Corwin joins me as I watch them drive off.

"They got a result", says Corwin.

"So the plan worked?", I enquire.

"Not exactly, but they got the desired result. Let's go to the Bucan now to get the full story."

Ten minutes later, we were sitting in the bar. Jean ordered champagne. The toast was to the "men of good intent". Each team member supplied their part of the story. The final part of the story was that Nesley had witnessed Beckham driving like a mad man, all over the road. At the right-hand bend, where they anticipated that he would lose control and fall into the ravine, he had miraculously managed to negotiate his way around but unfortunately for Beckham, coming the other way up Canapé Vert on the right side of the road was a four-ton camion. Nesley had seen the brake lights. The road surface was loose grit. The Dodge skidded but couldn't avoid a head-on collision with the camion. The camion driver was shaken. The Dodge driver was dead. Local people rendered what assistance they could until a UN patrol arrived and took control of the scene. The oughan's prediction had been fulfilled and the roads of Haiti had claimed another victim.

About two weeks after these events I was in my usual haunt, the bar St. Pierre, sipping on an early-evening frosted Prestige when I saw Jeslyn enter the bar. She greets me warmly. Through Mirelle the bar staff, I tell her that her looks have improved since I last saw her. She laughs. Over her shoulder I see Adz approaching. He slid his hand around her waist and said, "Hello Mr Chris. I must thank you for Jeslyn". I was hit with a wave of emotion. The three of us hugged.

I heard Mirelle say "If you want champagne, I'll send Madeline to get it".

"Get it", I replied.

Men of Good Intent

Chapter 15

MADAME OTTILIE, MARK AND MADAME FELICIA

I am a regular frequenter of the Bar St. Pierre. A permanent fixture who seats herself on a bar stool near the entrance is a woman who I now know to be Madame Ottilie. She just sits and keeps herself to herself. Everyone who passes by politely bids her "bon swa", but she rarely replies or speaks to anyone. The proprietor of Bar St. Pierre told everyone that she has been coming in every evening for some months now. She sits, sometimes she cries but he doesn't know why.

A few days ago I entered the bar and Madame Ottilie was in situ. That night she was dressed in white, from her head scarf to her shoes, not in her usual casual clothes. I guessed that she may have been to a funeral. As I passed by I bid her "bon swa" and tried to express condolences. To my surprise, she answered me in perfect English.

"Thank you, Mister Chris, (I had no idea she knew my name) it was not a funeral but the anniversary of my brother's death; I also mourn the loss of my other brother," she said sadly.

I said that I was sorry to hear that, and she went on to tell me the story.

Her brother André had married a local Haitian girl. After a few years the relationship had started to break down. He told his wife that he wanted a divorce. So one year ago to the day, Madame Ottilie and André were at Madame Ottilie's house when the wife's two brothers burst through the door. They shot André dead right in front of her. As they walked out they said to her "Here is his divorce". Madame Ottilie and her other brother Fabien informed the police. They advised her that they would investigate, providing that they were paid 200USD in investigation fees.

They scraped and borrowed to find the 200USD, which they duly paid to the police. Weeks went by and they heard nothing, so Fabien contacted the officer who was conducting the "investigation". The officer advised him that he had carried out 500USD worth of investigations and that they owed him a further 300USD! Fabien said that they could not pay. He was promptly arrested and conveyed to the prison in Port-au-Prince, where he remains to this day!

"So you see Mr Chris, why I'm lost. Haiti is a cruel country."

I sat there transfixed by her slow, deliberate, tearful delivery of her tale. I was choked with emotion. I offered to pay for her drink but she declined. She said "Please leave me now, I will not talk again".

Last December I was given a business card by a Haitian man who had opened a new bar called Shooters in Pétion-Ville. I remember stopping by there some months later but it was closed. A few nights ago I was in the Bucan Bar with a bunch of the "usual suspects", i.e. local businessmen, UN security, and freelance security. We had gathered to celebrate, as the previous weekend there had been a reported 47 kidnappings and 11 murders in Pétion-Ville alone!

The reason for the celebration was that one of our number, Mel, who is bodyguard to a local businessman, had foiled an attempt to kidnap his employer. He had shot dead the two chimère attackers. The beer was flowing and we congratulated him, not only on surviving the ambush but also sending out the right message to the gangs! In our alcohol-buoyed atmosphere, someone suggested that we should move on to a bar called Shooters, as it would be appropriate for the occasion. The fact that they also now featured exotic dancers sealed the deal, so off we went!

About 10 or 12 of us bounced into Shooters. We were shown to a table and informed that the exotic dancers had been booked for a private party that night! Mel was at the head of the table and started to regale us once more with his story. He and his boss had been out boozing all day with some of the "usual suspects". When it was time to leave, Mel had driven a follow car as his boss preferred to drive his own vehicle. When they reached the junction of Delmas and Delmas 48, Mel spotted the two chimères dressed in regulation baggy T-shirts, baseball caps and big basketball boots. He saw them nod to each other and walk from either side of the road to the stationery line of cars. He thought that they had targeted the boss, but they started towards him. Mel said he experienced instant alcohol evaporation.

We all drive with our handguns cocked and between our legs. He saw the chimère approach his driver's door and he saw the gun in his hand. Mel already had his gun in his hand and resting on his thigh, pointing towards the chimère. He also saw the other chimère at the passenger door. As he puts it, the next thing he knew he saw the snout of the chimère gun. By now he had fired twice through the skin of the door. Instantly dropping chimère number one. He says he must have turned and "double tapped" (shot twice) chimère number two, shattering the door window and scoring head shots and instant death. There was also a bullet hole in the roof of the car which he cannot account for.

He drove off and joined his boss who called his police SWAT squad (employed by his company). They attended the scene with PNH.

The crime scene investigation went like this:

PNH: "Did you shoot them?"

Mel: "Yes."

PNH: "Did they have guns?"

Mel: "Yes."

PNH: "OK, we'll get rid of the bodies."

With that, they commandeered a passing tap tap and ordered the driver to lose the bodies. Whilst we were enthralled by Mel's tale, I was aware of a Haitian woman who was standing back but listening intently. As he finished his story, the woman approached, shook Mel's hand and ordered drinks all round. She introduced herself as Madame Felicia and told us that she was the proprietor of Shooters. Her husband had been kidnapped, tortured and murdered four months ago and she had to pay a ransom to recover his dead body. Mel gave her a huge hug and we all promised to patronise her bar in future as a tribute to her husband. We did go back to Shooters but still haven't seen the exotic dancers!

Chapter 16

GOOD FUN!

Things are heating up! There is little news allowed out of Haiti by its interim government, due to the upcoming elections, as any adverse press would affect the international community's support. The UN Security Branch is the most reliable source of information. In fact one of our team members has a brother in UN Security, so we have a "hotline" into what's going on.

Haiti is supposed to be in a UN-designated "Post Conflict Phase". Pétion-Ville has a population of roughly 60,000. In the last month, kidnappings have been running at the rate of three per day, at least those are the ones we know of. Murders are about the same. Street robberies at gunpoint are countless. There are house invasions, where armed gangs kill the security guards and force the occupants out. The victims are middle class Haitians or expats. That's just a general overview of local crime, on top of that is the continuing battle against insurgent groups, mainly Lavalas (former supporters of president Aristide) and the FADH (Former Armi d'Haiti). The military was disbanded by the US when they reinstalled Aristide the second time.

The FADH have strongholds mainly in the north, at Gonaives and Cap Haitien, but they have cells which live amongst and enjoy the support of the people of the shanties of Cité Soliel, Kafou and

Bel Air. The UN troops carry out regular operations against them along the airport road and at Pont Rouge.

For all airport runs we now double up and take "longs" (long guns, US M4's). We had just completed an airport pick up and were on the airport road when my teammate, Arnie, receives a phone call from his brother, the UN contact. Arnie is saying "Yes, we're on the airport road near Behrmann Motors. Oh shit!". With that he drops his phone and puts his foot down, at the same time telling the passengers to get down, as we are about to pass a UN attack on FADH. Within seconds we are approaching the junction at Pont Rouge. I am front right in the vehicle, covering my arc which gives me a view down towards Batima. I see the UN Force, and at the same time the barrage opens up! I see a "50 cal", that is a 50 calibre machine gun, mounted on the back of a UN pickup truck, spitting fire and thudding away.

Simultaneously the small-arm fire response from the FADH cracks back. UN foot soldiers engage with automatic weapons. In a matter of seconds we are past the width of the junction and speeding off with the receding sounds of the battle behind us. I only got a glimpse of it and we were only in range for a few seconds, but we managed to escape any crossfire or stray shots!

Like I said before, this job is not just close protection. We also perform crowd control and loss prevention duties at the stores. At the Nazon store on the edge of Bel Air, we regularly have serious outbreaks of public disorder; crowds of a thousand or so will besiege the premises, fighting and surging in an effort to ransack the business. Our contract security guards use their shotgun butts to maintain order. When it really gets bad they fire a shot or two into the air, which may or may not restore tranquillity!

Last weekend I was detailed to go to a music event which the company was sponsoring, just off Rue John Brown. Over 50,000 people were expected, as Kreyol La were top of the bill. They are the top Kompa band in Haiti and they enjoy the same adulation and status as an international star. The company was also hosting an autograph signing by TeJo the lead singer. Then later the marketing team, consisting of three young men and four young women, were to give away T-shirts and goodies from the main stage. What could possibly go wrong? From my previous experience of such events the answer was, everything!

If there is anything that Haitians are passionate about, it is their music, and freebees. The autograph signing was manic. Stalls were pushed over, people got trampled, TeJo had his shirt ripped off. It was a hot and sweaty mess of adoration, but good fun. Then it was time for Kreyol La to perform and for the marketing team to be on stage, distributing the goodies into the crowd. Well, just getting the team on to the stage with their boxes of goodies intact whilst forging a way through the crowd was a major effort!

Kreyol La is on stage sound testing and tuning up for their set. The crowd is going crazy! The team decided to start throwing some goodies into the crowd. I can see people being crushed. The barrier around the pit at the front of the stage gives way under the weight of bodies. People flood forward and start climbing up onto the stage, grabbing at both goodies and at our team. Kreyol La is having difficulty tuning up now as the stage is being overrun. My teammate Sam and I corralled the marketing team to the back of the stage. The DJ is frantically screaming for security and police.

We order our team to climb down the scaffold to get to safety at the back of the stage, abandoning the boxes of goodies. The goodies quickly disappear into the crowd, where fights break out amongst those trying to retain their prized goodies and those trying to steal them. The stage clears. We gathered our marketing group together, ready to escort them back to their vehicle outside of the venue. I register that they are all wearing logo-bearing promotional clothing of T-shirts and baseball caps. I ascertain that all of them have no change of clothing. Sam and I confer. We agree on tactics to get us through the crowd. The simple plan is, as soon as Kreyol La starts up, we gather the marketing team to form up like a rugby scrum. Sam and I take the lead. On word of command "go", the marketing team throw their baseball caps to the right of the crowd as a distraction. Hopefully there will be a surge towards the flying caps, which might give us a break through the crowd and an opportunity to escape.

Kreyol La appears to be faffing, having difficulty getting started. The crowd is getting even more restless. Two shotgun blasts rent the air. This seems to have a galvanising effect on Kreyol, as they crank it up and the huge speakers deliver the first beats, which leave your internal organs vibrating! The crowd roars! The word "go" sees the caps flying, the crowd surging. We are off! As a group we force our way through the crowd, trying our best to cover the female team members as hands are grabbing at their T-shirts with logos. As we reach the edge of the crush the team are laughing their heads off, having got caught up in the euphoria of the event. A couple of girls had lost their T-shirts and were standing in nothing but jeans and bras!

The concert Is on and the fans are jumping In unison to the beat. The marketing team is safe; job well done! It's all in a day's work for us security men. The marketing team decided to rejoin the party. I look at Sam and he looks at me. We are both sweating heavily. Our job is done.

"St. Pierre?", I say.

"Exactly what I was thinking", replies Sam, as we set off to our favourite watering hole.

Chapter 17
WHAT IWAN WANTS

A nother busy week! We've been averaging between twelve to fifteen hours per day and are supposed to be working only six days a week, but the company is up for sale and thus we've had visitors who we were required to drive and protect. So, no time off. On other jobs that I have done in Iraq, Africa, Ukraine etc, once you have delivered your "pax" (as we refer to our principals), there is usually a "down room" where you can relax. Not on this job!

Apart from the "taxi service" we provide, there is the store security. Also at the Nazon store there is the public order situation, with mini riots regularly breaking out! Plus high-value load escorts and anything else we get tasked with, official or unofficial. Each day we receive our UN security briefs. Daily now the UN is in action on the airport road. Reports were circulating that some UN troops had been offering extra "security" to some of the businesses that operated along that road, at a price of course!

With all this on my mind, and having read a moderate threat level report, I had just dropped a pax off at the airport and was approaching the UN checkpoint to get onto the airport road proper. Concrete barriers are positioned so that you have to zigzag to enter and exit. As I slow down to negotiate the barriers, a UN Brazilian army corporal steps forward and indicates to me to stop. His partner, a private soldier about 20 years old, levels his rifle at me. I stop and lower my window. The corporal has his rifle slung across his chest and he indicates with his hands a gripping action, like a dog begging, so I grip the top of my steering wheel.

As he reaches my window he is snarling "Américains, Américains?".

I get the distinct impression that he is not a fan of the US. I guess if I speak English I could be in trouble. So I respond in my best Kreyol inflection:

"Non, non, Ayee shi en" (this is how the locals pronounce Haitian).

He responds "No Américains!".

He then makes a beckoning gesture with his fingers.

I say "papiers?", and raising my right hand off the wheel I look at him. He nods. I reach into my back pocket, take out my wallet and produce my Haitian driving licence and NIC card (identity and residency permit). He examines my two cards, sneers and hands them back to me. In the process of taking out my wallet I had to move my vest back, exposing my hand gun. The corporal says "Zam", so I slowly take out my gun, release the magazine and clear my weapon. As I am doing this he trains his rifle on me.

"Papiers", he says, so I show him my police weapon permit.

"OK, OK", says the corporal.

I reload and replace my gun in my holster. The corporal seems a little disappointed. He is just looking at me now and prattling on in Portuguese, however I do pick out "Fuck Américains", which he repeats several times. He starts to pat his pockets and points at me.

I say "pa compron". He raises his voice, pats his pockets more vigorously and points at me. I gather that he either wants to search me or for me to give him some money or something. I raise my voice to drown his.

"Mw Ayee si en, pa gen Américains, pou ki sa ou pwoblem por mw?" (I am Haitian, not American. Why do you give me problems?).

I guess that he has no idea what I am talking about and that I must be one of the arrogant light-skinned Haitian Mulatto. Because with that he signals to the private to lower his rifle and waves me through. It's bad enough that the local cops are corrupt but with the UN at it as well?

Talking about the police, two hundred cops have been fired in the last week in the Port-au-Prince/Pétion-Ville precincts, in an attempt to get rid of the corrupt ones. Trouble is they have been allowed to keep their uniforms and guns. Also at the same time a number of police cars have disappeared.

Iwan is one of our technicians, he is about 35 years old and, shall we say, nature had an off day when it handed out physical features? He'd been working late. I had just collected him to take him to his apartment.

Iwan speaks reasonable English, and we are having some chit-chat when he says, "I want to do something".

I respond with "Go shopping, have a drink?".

Iwan repeats, "No, no, something".

"Eat?"

Iwan says yet again, "Something".

"Iwan you will have to tell me"

"I want to fuck!"

I remind him of the rules. We are not allowed to take clients to brothels. Iwan tells me that he has been here for two months now without "comfort". Well I look at him, I am flooded with compassion so I relent. I pull up outside the "Soft Lady" club. I call the armed security guard over, slip him 25 gourdes and ask him to look after my friend. I watch Iwan disappear into the bowels of the "Soft Lady". I lower the back rest of my car seat and look up at the digital clock, it reads 2204 hours. I settle back for the wait. I'm internally cursing myself for allowing this. Why did I relent? I have to be up at 0600 hours. Too late now, it is done.

I am still gazing in the dark at the clock when I see Iwan smoking a cigarette and heading back to the car. The clock reads 2213 hours.

"Problem?", I ask.

Iwan says, "No, I'm good".

"OK, let's get you home", I say.

I do the mental arithmetic; it had taken just 9 minutes, which includes entering the premises, completing negotiations, doing the deed, walking out and smoking a cigarette. Not such a late night after all.

Chapter 18
MAXIMUM SECURITY

A t night the streets of Pétion-Ville are dark; the only illumination comes from passing cars, bars, hotels, discos, restaurants and brothels. There are occasional burning mounds of rubbish smouldering away by the roadside. The people of the night gather at these points of light.

"Maximum security", that's the unofficial vehicle parking protection racket that flourishes outside of these establishments. It's run by Alex and Nickson, who both work their patch outside the St Pierre bar. For a few gourdes they will look after your car and offer you their "bitches", at extra cost of course! Their "bitches" are the street prostitutes, known locally as "coco-rats" (coco is local slang for vagina, rats = rats). If you are a devotee of Russian roulette then you might consider playing with your health. Actually, if you take the time to get to know some of these characters and once they know that you are not interested, they don't bother you too much. You can just exchange banter, gather local intelligence and have a bit of fun.

The elections are supposed to be upcoming soon. The police that were fired a couple of weeks ago have been replaced by cops from the provinces. There has been publicity in the media that the streets would be cleaned up, in preparation for the world's press who will attend for the run up to the election.

Last Friday night I was driving back to my apartment after an evening in the St Pierre bar. I turned into one of the interconnecting side roads off Rue Rebecca when I was confronted by two police trucks blocking the way. There were six cops. Two were standing back giving armed cover while two others were busy with their rifle butts working over four coco-rats. By now I had stopped.

A corporal who was in charge approached me.

"UN, UN?", he asked.

I just shrugged. I was more intent on watching the brutality. At this point a young man was dragged out of one of the police trucks and thrown on the ground. I saw a cop draw his hand gun, point it at the man's head and fire twice. I was stunned. The man just lay there and I could see his body trembling. The corporal was standing next to me laughing!

I couldn't believe what I had just seen. "Mesyer, mw protest?", I said.

The corporal said "pa gen pwoblem masisi, pa gen mori".

I couldn't make out much more of what he said but I gathered that the man was gay and had just been given a fright. The cop had fired either side of his head! The prisoners were bundled into the police trucks and I was waved through. The corporal thumped his chest and said "Remen travay mw, bye" (I love my job, bye!).

Our DG (Director General) was having dinner at a client's house on Musso last Saturday night. The DG is a big man physically who has worked all over the world, setting up all kinds of businesses; not the kind of man who scares easily. It was about 2130 hours when we received a call that there had been sustained automatic gun fire close to where he was and that he wanted out.

Sam and I were tasked to go and recce (and draw fire?). I was the driver and Sam was the "shooter", sitting in the back with an M4 rifle.

We drove up Musso which is an area with jungle on one side and nice houses behind walls with security on the other. Our UN source had no intelligence on that area. The house we sought was at the end of a road, which became a track which led into the jungle. We parked just inside the edge of the jungle, switched off our engine, wound the windows down and listened. We stayed like that for 20 minutes. We heard nothing untoward, just the night-time jungle sounds. Al and Trev were detailed to do the pick up. We watched as they drove up to the gates. The guards let them in. A few minutes later they emerged with the DG on board. They turned right down the hill. I started the engine, turned on the lights and fell in behind them.

We had only gone about 100 metres when we heard "Cracracracracrak". Close by! The distinctive sound of automatic gunfire split the night. Instinctively we ducked, throttled hard down, switched the vehicle lights off and set off at speed! I was right up the backside of the lead car as we hurtled down the slope. We rounded a right-hand bend, which put us behind a high wall and cover. The lead car put its lights back on and slowed to a safer speed. I did the same. We were clear. The whole incident was over in seconds and no one had sustained a hit! We took the DG home.

At least he knows what he is paying for now!

Chapter 19

JWAYE NWEL (MERRY CHRISTMAS)

There are no public toilets in Pétion-Ville! All liquid waste of whatever nature runs along the side of the roads, together with household, human and animal solids. Men and women urinating at the side of the road are a frequent sight. Most are discrete but there is an element of arrogant young men who make an aggressive show of it.

The women here carry all loads on their heads. It is quite impressive to see a woman with a huge load on her head casually gather up her skirt, squat and pee, without dropping her load! If urinating is common, defecation in the street is more discrete and usually takes place in accepted locations which are generally out of common sight. However one can work out where they are by the "aroma"!

Since the "Christmas Promotion" which started on 5th December, the situation at the stores has dangerously deteriorated. All the stores have had substantial disorder, ranging from pushing and shoving to guns being drawn and shots fired. We have employed our own PNH to police our crowds. So along with our daily missions of armed escorting of our clients through "kidnap alley", we are trying to avoid the UN's daily shooting practice on the way! On top of that there have been evening "Christmas

Dinner" runs, after we have spent our days wrestling with mobs trying to access the stores!

We were averaging 16 to 18 hours per day, with no days off. All team members are more than a little beat. The crowds are not particularly directing violence at us personally, they just want to get in to get their phones. People begin to queue outside stores in the early hours of the morning, so by the time we open for business at around 0900 hours, up to 800 or more people have been waiting for 5 or 6 hours, with no toilet facilities under the searing sun!

So, after our transports, we start our days pressed up against writhing, sweating bodies, not all in the highest states of hygiene. People gabbling and ranting in your face, with breath smells from teeth that have no knowledge of toothpaste and a brush! It is just like working the door of a crazy night club. Could it be the years I spent doing that were not wasted? It's physically draining work, because your own body is constantly under pressure from the sheer mass of others' bodies weighing upon you.

There were too many incidents to mention. About a week before I was at the Rue Frere store, where we had erected a canopy on some wasteland at a distance from the store in an effort to keep the bulk of people away from the front door. Most people were patiently waiting in the shade, out of the reach of the blazing sun. An altercation broke out at the front of the queue involving about 20 people. I'm not sure what sparked it, probably people pushing in. I stood back to let my contract security guard deal with it but Haitian "conflict management" skills are still in their infancy. The situation went from chaos to life-threatening in seconds!

The guard, after screaming and shouting for a few seconds ineffectually, went straight up the "force continuum". He racked his pump-action shotgun and pointed it above the heads of the mob. Unfortunately this did not have the effect that he had hoped for, because the mob continued to advance towards him. Those at the front are less eager than those at the back! Mob hysteria had taken over and they were closing on the panicking guard. He levelled his weapon at the advancing hysterical mass. I'm now running towards the guard, approaching from his left side. I get to his side with the mob about 10 feet away but closing fast. I am shouting, "T'bak, t'bak!" and have my hands at head height, making a double-handed pressing motion with my palms to the crowd.

I can see in the guard's eyes that he is going to fire.

Instinctively, I grab the barrel of his shotgun and force it down. I continue to face the crowd, continuing to signal to them with my left hand and shouting "prosey, prosey, dousman" (easy, easy, steady). The mob falters, the front few are now standing uncertainly just in front of me and the guard. Those at the back were urging forward. I wrest the gun from the hands of the guard and proceed to give him an almighty bollocking! Unfortunately I don't think that he or the crowd understood what I was saying because it was all in English! However there are certain expletives that are internationally recognised. The message must have gotten across because the crowd calmed down. The trembling guard looked sheepish and a bloodbath was averted.

Chapter 20
POLITICS AND PROSTITUTES!

Slogans and posters of the thirty-three candidates are everywhere. Nightly, pickup trucks full of supporters with music and loud hailers trundle around the streets, followed by mobs. When two opposing factions meet, the inevitable "manifestation" happens. Vehicles are turned over, there's stoning and fighting, barricades are erected with surprising speed, cars are dragged across the street and set on fire. Shots fired!

We have had our own riots to contend with. Last month the company launched its GSM system (Global System for Mobile communications) for a minimum price of 90USD. As of the 5th of December their Christmas promotion started, which means that you can now buy this same system for only 30USD! The marketing department anticipated a massive sales boost. In fact, all those who paid 90USD are less than chuffed, and have turned out in force to protest! So, combined with all those trying to get the 30USD deal, as well as the protesters, we have a volatile cocktail. The Martissant store has come under sustained gun fire. The Nazon store was overrun and sacked! I was at a less lively venue on Rue Frere but even there we had fistfights and security letting off a few rounds in order to gain control!

It was just after lunch on Wednesday and I was making a phone call to the UK, so I had momentarily moved away from the crowd. I saw a group of half a dozen youths, all wearing red bandanas around their heads (L.A. gangsta style). It wasn't so much the bandanas which attracted me but the machetes they were carrying! I got to the door before them. I joined Sam, my team mate. Our local contract security had locked themselves inside the store!

The crowd became subdued. I could hear mutterings of "Chimère, Chimère". This little team swaggered up to us. The leader, a short skinny man about 25 years old and dressed for basketball, stepped towards me and said,

"Blan, Chimère mw."

I replied "Chimère, pou ki sa?" (what is that?).

The chimère sneered, gabbled something I couldn't understand and raised his machete towards me. I said "Pa gen suk natu koupe isit?" (no sugar cane to cut here?). Suppressed laughter seeped out from the crowd.

"Te machett mwe" (I am little machett), said the chimère.

"Mwe zamm ampil" (I'm big gun), I replied.

He contemplated me then gave that derisive, threatening teeth suck which is common among Africans. He then sneered "bloo fair" (bluffer). I am told my Kreyol is quite convincing because I can mimic the stuttering cadence and mannerisms required to sound authentic. I stared back at him, "sucked" and said "poss eeb?" (maybe). There was a moment of tension then; I can only assume that I "out sucked" him, because he turned and snarled something to his troops. They then broke into a chant and rhythmically jog-trotted off, waving their machetes as they went!

It was about 1700 hours and getting dark that same night when I picked up a client whom I shall refer to as "A". He told me that he had some personal business to attend to. He went on to tell me that he had fallen for a Dominican Republic prostitute. He had released her from her contract at the Soft Lady Club by paying 500USD to the club management. Some confusion had arisen when "A" went home on leave. On his return she was missing. He had just received a phone call from her to say that she had been abducted from the street and was now held as a sex slave in the Soft Lady. The management had seized her passport. Could he rescue her by paying a further 500USD?

I did advise him as to the possible problems he could find himself with. However he was adamant that he at least wanted to see her.

"A" is a senior figure in the company and knows the rules about visiting brothels. He didn't want me to compromise myself by taking him to one. I dropped him off at the Western Union office in the same street, which was where he was to be if anyone asked. I watched him pass through the security and into the innards of the Soft Lady. I had to drive around the block. By now it was quite dark so I pulled up opposite the entrance of the club. The street was thronging with people and cars. I don't think that the Soft Lady security was aware of me.

After 20 minutes I received a phone call from "A".

"The management wants 1,000USD and I don't have it."

I advised him where I was and that he should just get out before they kidnap him too! A few minutes later I see "A" framed in the club doorway with a female hugging him. Just at that point gunfire shatters the air about 50 metres away. The people on the street duck as one, as if being swiped by a giant hand. Soft Lady security raise their shotguns, moving towards the shooting. "A" and his girlfriend are crouched down running towards my car. I open the back door and they dive onto the seat, lying flat. I put my foot down and joined the cars speeding away from the shooting. Within a few seconds we were out of sight of the Soft Lady and their security, heading to "A"s house and safety. The plan now was that DR girl would not leave "A"s house without security, report her passport lost to her embassy and apply for a new one. "A"s house has four armed security guards. She will be safe.

Chapter 21

THE CURSE OF EL GATO NEGRO!

I like Fernando. He is one of our key workers. He is the man who goes out into the wilds where the company has its antennae. He climbs the structures, wrestles with the microwave dish and gets it all to connect up and work. He is in his late twenties, from Argentina and is a bit of a loose cannon in as much as if he has to get a job done he will, without any authority, get on and do it. Whatever means to the end. Which ensures that he is a security nightmare, but the DG loves him because he makes it all happen so business can grow. Due to his cavalier, pioneering nature he has been involved in many incidents during the two years that he has been here. This has earned him the nickname of "El Gato Negro" (the black cat), which in Latin America equates to "the cat with nine lives".

I received the message from Arnie: "Pack your bags, you're going down the coast with Fernando, be prepared for at least two nights out". So, with kit packed and happy to be getting out into the provinces, away from the craziness of Port-au-Prince, I picked up Fernando and Evon (our Haitian guide and Fernando's assistant). We set out on Route Nationale 2 heading towards the coast. The first hurdle was to negotiate our way through Kafou. I've mentioned before just how bad the squalor of Kafou is. We are driving along the open sewer which serves as the main road, past dead bodies lying by the roadside amongst the piled-up rubbish. Eventually we break out of the greater Port-au-Prince city limits onto a reasonable stretch of coastal road, which looks more like how the Carribean should look! After about two hours of driving the road gives way to tracks and now we are truly doing "off roading". The Hyundai is bouncing along, happily crossing rivers where the bow wave washes up the windscreen! We are passing rural scenes that have not changed in centuries, subsistence farmers working the land with animals.

We reach a point, according to Fernando's GPS (Global Positioning System) where we have to strike out into the interior and drive up a mountain trail. This means we are now following ancient footpaths and animal tracks. After about another hour of neck-jerking driving through primary jungle, where we only see the occasional 4-wheel drive vehicle. my mind starts to wander back to when I was a boy in the late 1950's, early 60's and watching the old black and white television programs of adventure and exploration. I recall old monochrome 1950's television nature programs of Aramand and Michaela Dennis exploring "Darkest Africa". Well, here I was all these years later living it! We stopped by a local hut and bought some grilled corn.

Fernando and Evon are chomping away as I continue to drive. The corn smells good. I am hungry. Fernando suggests we swap places so that I can eat corn and he can drive. It did occur to me that he is "el gato negro" and that he does have a reputation. But I was hungry and we were miles from anywhere. What could possibly go wrong? Fernando is enjoying himself off-roading. "This is fun", he laughs. We start to ascend a winding path up the Montagn La Pilon. Fernando's driving confidence is growing! He is pushing on. I look out of my window and see a drop of about 100 feet. I tell Fernando to ease up.

We round a bend and Fernando just keeps going straight ahead. I watch in horror as he drives us straight over the edge of the precipice! I don't know if he braked or what but we stopped suddenly with a jolt! The engine died. The car is just short of a 45 degree angle in my direction, hanging over the cliff edge! I look to my right and I am looking straight down into a valley 100-plus feet below.

I shout to Fernando, "Get out, get out!".

He is just sitting looking ahead muttering, "What happened?".

I'm pushing him, applying the handbrake, putting the car in neutral gear, opening Fernando's door all at the same time. Evon reacts a little faster and jumps out. I am scrambling, pushing Fernando out of the car. The next thing that I know is that we are standing on the track, looking at my Hyundai perched ready to topple over the edge! Fernando is transfixed, just staring at the car.

I turn to him and say calmly, "How did you manage that?".

He continues to stare ahead and replies, "Where did the road go?".

I feel quite elated, the fact that we are alive and standing looking at what should have been our demise.

I turn to him and say, "The curse of el gato negro?".

I go over to Evon who is shaking and sitting against the side of the mountain. I tell him that he needs some exercise to calm down and tell him to run to the village that we passed a mile or so back down the track and get some help in the form of a camion (big truck), able bodies and some strong rope. So, we sit and wait patiently, exchanging pleasantries. Fernando couldn't explain why he had driven off the side of the cliff! A boulder directly beneath our front right wheel had saved us. There we sat for about two hours, much to the amusement of local hill people who just laughed at the crazy "blans" driving off the cliff. By now some ten local people had gathered, they obviously wanted to see how we were going to get out of this one!

Eventually we hear the approaching grumbling of the oldest four ton Mercedes truck imaginable! It came to a halt in front of us hissing steam. Miki, the owner/driver introduced himself to us and explained how he will "save" us. At this point another tap tap camion trundles up the track with twenty or more passengers on the back. They all jump off, eager to help. Ropes are produced, one tied to the front left towing bracket. Two ropes are tied around the rear bumper bar to prevent the back end from swinging out and falling. The front rope is attached to the Mercedes and the other two ropes are being pulled on by ten locals per rope. My job is to stand on the running board, hold the steering wheel and release the hand brake. I was in a position where I could jump onto the track if the car was to fall. I signal to Miki and call out "dousman" (steady). He revs the Merc, the rope tightens and the pullers on the rope call out a cadence. I shout "Un, du, twa". The Merc shudders backwards, we lurch forward and to the left onto the track. The force of the pull propels my car forward towards the front of the Merc. I lean in to pull on the hand brake. The suddenness of the movements cause me to pitch into the open window. I grab the hand brake, stopping us from colliding with the front of the Merc, which would have meant an accident report.

I am now arse up in the air, my legs sticking out of the driver's side door window. This meets with the approval of the pullers and onlookers as a peal of laughter goes up! Hands grab me and pull me from the car. Much hand shaking and congratulations takes place. After a few minutes of elation, I still have my car in one piece and I won't have any awkward explaining to do. I look at Fernando who is standing well back and a little sheepish. I call out to him "Get yer wallet out!"; 200USD lighter but with relief we get back into the car.

Fernando says it first: "You drive".

I ask, "How much farther to the site?".

After some discussion amongst our local help and lots of pointing, in the opposite direction! We realise that we needn't have gone on this track in the first place!

Chris Nott

CALL SIGN CHOPPER-THE SEQUEL

CALL SIGN CHOPPER-THE SEQUEL

Chris Nott

CALL SIGN CHOPPER-THE SEQUEL

Chapter 22
THE CURSE CONTINUES!

W ell, we eventually got onto the right track. Fernando was not happy because we had fallen well behind schedule and it was all his own fault. We are now climbing up a track which had recently been cut to facilitate access to the antennae up on top of the mountain. I have the Hyundai Terracan in 4-wheel drive, low mode. We are making hard progress, the incline increases sharply, the track surface changes to loose shale on top of sand. The 4-wheel drive just can't cope with it and the wheels spin, throwing up dust. We sink to our axles, slide backwards and come to a halt. We get out to examine our situation and we find that the car is resting on its axles in the sand. Any attempt to drive out results only in wheels spinning and dust clouds. Fernando is furious. We can see the antennae in the distance, maybe two miles away.

Fernando and I make the decision. It is imperative that he gets the work done on the antennae, so he and Evon start humping their kit out of the car and strike out on foot. We are near the top of a mountain. The few locals we meet appear friendly so I stay with the car and see what I can do, hopefully to join them later. After repeated attempts to get moving, which involve much digging around the wheels and using the mats, combined with lots of sweating, realisation dawns that I am not going to be able to move without getting help from someone. So, I get out my Thermos flask of tea, my Tupperware sandwich box, make myself comfortable in the driver's seat, enjoy my picnic and watch the sun dipping towards the horizon!

If it weren't for my predicament, it would have been a pleasant late afternoon and evening. I try calling the office via the sat phone (satellite phone) but get no reply. So what to do? I had enough food and water for two days. I was six hours away from Port-au-Prince and any help from other team members, so I settled down for the night. After about half an hour a small boy appeared, wandering down the mountain. I ascertained that he lived up higher and that he could get help. Another half an hour passes by and three men appear. They are equipped with shovels, rope and a donkey! After lots of excavating and beating of the donkey, which had a rope tied to its girdle to pull while the men pushed and me throttling the Terracan, I am still just as stuck as I was before, but 200 gourdes lighter in the wallet! The sun is approaching the horizon. We all sit around helplessly. The donkey wanders off in a huff! In the distance we hear a rumbling noise, the unmistakable sound of a big diesel engine. It hoves into view, another ancient four ton Mercedes truck!

The first attempt at towing me out fails. The driver decides that more weight is required, so the flatbed is loaded up with rocks. When the load looks about right we get set for another go. I'm revving the engine, stones fly! The three men pushing, the Merc groaning. I suddenly feel the purchase. To the sounds of cheering, the Merc pulls me forward and we don't stop but keep going until we reach a plateau about a quarter of a mile on up. The Merc driver assures me that I will be able to make it from there. I give him a 100USD bill, which he is happy with. I make it up to the site where the antenna is situated on top of the mountain.

Fernando is 100-odd feet up the antennae, working away. Eventually he comes down, having fixed the problem.

Fernando has to go to another site at Jeremie which is a further three-hour drive through friendly territory. I am advised that if the Terracan wouldn't make it up this hill, it wouldn't get to the Jeremie site. Fernando leaves with the construction team and I stay with the two other workers to head back to Port-au-Prince when they finish work. I get through on the sat phone and am told to return to Port-au-Prince with the contractors. The two Ecuadorian contractors get to work. At about 2300 hours they decide that they have had enough, so we settle down to sleep for the night. I have a sleeping bag and find a place to spend the night in the half-built compound. I have an uncomfortable night, as there was no escape from the generator noise! In the morning I pay a small boy aged about 8 years, 10 gourdes for a couple of chunks of ginger bread which he is selling to the construction workers. His mother comes over and explains that I am the first real live blan that he has ever seen. She shows me an old tatty French magazine with white people in it. The boy looks at me in awe! The contractors work all day and into the evening. We leave at about 1900 hours and get back to Port-au-Prince by about 0100 hours, after a relatively uneventful drive.

The next day our management decided that we should go out to Fernando as we have an obligation to protect him. So Dan and myself set out, this time in a Nissan Patrol which we are assured can tackle any terrain. We retrace our route to the turning point for Jeremie. At this stage we make contact via cellphone with Fernando. The time is 1500 hours. He advises us that he is now moving to Les Cayes so we make arrangements to meet him at the site there. At about 1730 hours we approach Les Cayes. For the last two hours we have not had a cellphone signal. My phone rings. It's Fernando, he's in Port-au-Prince! He got to Les Cayes, fixed the problem in two minutes flat and went to a local airfield, just in time to get a flight back to Port-au-Prince. Dan and I find a hotel that unfortunately has no food! So we explore and discover a beach side shack. We enjoy some local fare and a beer or three!

Chapter 23
SKULLS, DIRTY TRICKS AND GUNFIRE

The last few weeks have been the calmest that I have known in all the time that I have been out here. The airport runs are less eventful, kidnappings are down, shootings sporadic. However there is always something to keep you on your toes! A couple of weeks ago there were discoveries of human skulls at various locations around Pétion-Ville. The first was a set of twelve clean skulls in a diamond pattern, which appeared on Rue Metellus by the roadside, directly opposite our director general's house. The next was seventeen skulls, also laid out in diamond formation, discovered the following day on Canapé Vert, on the run-up to the company's main offices. The third and final skull discovery was on Rue Pinchinat, on the lead-up to the company's new offices, where lay 22 clean human skulls! The UN police were on the scene of each discovery. I tried to take some photographs at the Canapé Vert site, but was refused by a UN cop from Burkina Faso, who told me it was a crime scene.

I got chatting with an American cop. I asked him if they had made any local enquiries to contact the *oughan* (Vodou priest) for the area. He told me that he didn't believe in any of that bullshit and that this was a straightforward murder investigation. He wasn't prepared to accept that the skulls may have come from local graveyards and could be some kind of Vodou message.

Competition is coming! The biggest cellphone company in the Caribbean is out to make a killing here in Haiti. Research has shown that Haitians, although some of the poorest people in the world, have the highest per capita cellphone usage. So the race is on to win the "prize" of the "cell phone jewel in the Caribbean". The potential profits to be had are huge! Just lately the company has experienced a series of problems with network crashes and attacks on outlying installations by mobs. These events have coincided with the rival company entering the fray. Dirty tricks? Industrial sabotage? Could it be? Our DG is paranoid! Let's see what unfolds!

It was Matt's birthday. He is one of our seniors, generally regarded as being a bit of a "plonker" by some team members. Anyway he throws out an invitation to his birthday party at the Basilic restaurant to the whole team, and he is footing the bill! Well, he may be a "plonker", but who cares? Six of us turned up for our free binge. At the same time at Café Albert, our DG was hosting a dinner for visiting company majority shareholders from the US. I was on my second Prestige. On the label of the bottle are two words: Prestige bière. No health warnings, calorific contents, advice to drink sensibly, etc! Suddenly, the skirl of bagpipes split the Caribbean night. It was Arnie's cellphone ringtone! After a couple of seconds listening, Arnie says, "We're on our way". We are on our toes and running. Arnie explains that heavy automatic gunfire has been reported, just outside the entrance to Café Albert.

We jump into our motors, all six of our Terracans screaming down the track, headlights full beam, to dazzle any oncoming vehicles. We get onto the road and spread across it, forcing anything coming the opposite way into the sewer ditches on either side. We see a couple of sets of headlights in front of us, which turn into rear lights as they perform reversing manoeuvres, then speed off. We stop about 100 metres short of Café Albert and take up positions around Plas Boyer Parc, making sure that our "arcs of fire" interlock. Arnie is on the radio and cellphone to Tad, the DG's bodyguard. The plan is that he will go forward with Darryl whilst we cover them. The DG and his party will get into their armoured car and we will make a coordinated extraction at speed, which is exactly what happened. I dived back into my car as the "hard" car containing the DG approached me, and I followed on giving rear cover. No further gunfire is heard. It must have been a little local domestic strife! We get out of the area and take the party to the Montana Hotel, where they resume their celebrations. We race back to the Basilic and Matt's shindig, only to find that the waitresses and chefs have eaten our meals! Food certainly doesn't go to waste out here.

Chapter 24

WE WAIT

P ierre (Haitian teammate) and I are locked in at the Nazon store, along with our five contract security guards, who are each armed with .38 revolvers and pump-action shotguns. We have food and drink for three days, which should be enough if we are locked in for the duration. Dawn is breaking, historically the time when attacks occur. So far all is quiet, that is apart from the distant drumming which drifts on the smokey air out of the slum of Bel Air. Today, Tuesday the 7th of February, 2006 is election day! The first free presidential elections to be held here in recent times, under the organisation and auspices of the UN. World history in the making? The run up to this momentous occasion has been turbulent. So, why am I sitting here in combat kit with my M4 assault rifle, CZ handgun and 3,000 rounds of ammo?

The Nazon store is situated on the road (which is really nothing more than a track) that divides the slums of Salines and Bel Air, where opposing chimère gangs battle it out. Bel Air has had a period of relative calm after residents rose up against the gangs and killed some of them. "Jungle law" replaces one gang with another. The Salinas gangs, opportunistically ready to exploit the disarray in Bel Air, fired a few warning shots of intention. At times of public upheaval, American interests have come under attack. The Nazon store is the biggest building in the district which is owned by an American company. So, we sit and wait.

Pierre is on patrol, checking the guards who are visibly nervous. We noticed that they were wearing T-shirts underneath their uniforms. They say it's cold. The real reason for this is, should there be any rioting, and it looks like we will be overrun, they could then discard their uniform shirts and blend into the crowds and disappear! Effectively, we are on our own, Pierre and I. The rest of the team are similarly deployed at other locations. Sporadic distant gunfire joins the drumming on the smokey air.

So, we sit and wait.

Chapter 25
SIX THOUSAND VOICES

When it came it was through a shimmering heat haze. We received a telephone call from UN Intelligence: "A manifestation (mob) from Bel Air is heading your way intent on havoc". Pierre trained the surveillance cameras on the approach road, but there was nothing. I went outside, it was 1100 hours and the sun was high. I looked into the sun up the Nazon Road.

I heard it before I saw it. The rhythmic slapping of 12,000 sandaled/flip-flopped feet, accompanied by the chanting of 6,000 voices, all combined with the heat haze to create a palpable throbbing, reverberating through the slum valley of Nazon. The head of the mob emerged out of the haze, drawing menacingly closer. Pierre and I grabbed our M4's and went to our stand to positions.

Our security guards couldn't escape, as we had used our vehicles to barricade the gates. So they had no option but to adopt defensive positions. The front runners of the mob could be clearly seen now, some carrying machetes and some brandishing handguns. I couldn't make out their chant.

Pierre translated: "If Preval is not president, the bourgeois will die". The leaders were now within 200m of the south gate, the volume and intensity growing with each jogged step.

Pierre instructed the guards not to fire until he ordered it. We each trained our rifles on the armed men in the mob and waited. As the head of the mob reached the south gate, the chant became disjointed. I could pick out the words "Américains" and "mouri" (death). Sections of the mob were gesturing towards our building, waving machetes and letting off a few shots into the air. I was soaked in sweat and my body armour was gripping me like a vice. The main bulk of the mob processed past us, slinging a few insults and more sky-destined shots.

After what must have been only a matter of seconds but seemed like minutes, it dawned on us that we were not the target of the mob's intent. We had received no effective fire or any attempt to storm the gates. We maintained our positions and watched and waited as the mob passed by. This went on for several minutes. As the stragglers and the less athletic ones ambled or limped past us, we were aware that the fabric of the building had received no hits and none of us was hurt. We stood down from our positions and went inside, taking off our sweat-saturated body armour.

"Fancy a coffee?", I said to Pierre.

"Oui", he said.

Chapter 26

NO MORE REVERSING!

It started out as a good day with beautiful sunshine. I had completed all my runs and the clients were all securely housed. I decided to take a little time for myself and grab a coffee back at the apartment before my next mission. I'm driving up Rue John Brown, where directly in front of me is an old white Toyota pick-up truck. I get to a point just past the junction with Dalencourt when, for no apparent reason, the Toyota stops and starts to roll back towards me. There are no exhaust emissions and no exhaust pipe vibrations visible to indicate that the engine is running. I stop and sound my horn, but the Toyota keeps coming. I look in my mirror and see that the road is clear to my rear. I slap my vehicle into reverse and start edging backwards, looking over my right and left shoulders, to my front and in my mirror. I see a white car emerging from a junction to my left rear. The Toyota keeps on coming, I am now positioned in the middle of the junction. I look over my right shoulder: clear. Look over my left shoulder: CRUNCH!!!

I apply the hand brake. As I'm looking forward, the Toyota spurts a cloud of smoke from the exhaust, turns right to drive off down Dalencourt and is lost to sight! The vehicle with which I had collided was a Jeep from the US embassy. He had tried to slip in behind me to go down Dalencourt. After much arm waving and loud voices, information is exchanged. Fortunately the local traffic control cops are on hand. They stand around in a group watching in amusement. The good thing is that, with the feared cops on the scene, the gathering crowd kept their distance. Our Haitian fleet manager attends, formalities are completed, and I can continue on my way. I told you already about Haitian driving. Well my view of the accident is that the Toyota had overshot the right turn into Dalencourt, so he just switched off his engine to roll back to turn right! No other considerations in his mind, he just had to turn right.

I have to collect a client and take him on site visits. Pylons are being constructed around Pétion-Ville to facilitate full cell phone coverage. Rodrigues is responsible for building progress and makes daily visits to motivate the Haitian workers. I told Rodrigues about my road traffic accident (RTA). He is mildly amused but shrugs his shoulders. "That's just the way it is here." We check out his sites as usual, but there's not a lot of progress. Rodrigues is not best pleased, so he directs me to go to the last site where concrete was due to be poured that day. This site is situated off a rough track, off Pellerin nine, on the Kenscoff Road, up the side of Montagn Noir (Black Mountain). It is particularly difficult to get to. In fact all materials including water had to be manhandled up there, an arduous task.

Only 4-wheel drive vehicles can make it there and even then it is a torturous drive. At one point there is a sharp hairpin bend and on the outer edge of this turn is a sheer drop of 200 feet. The edges of the track regularly crumble away. So, the usual practice when negotiating this bend is for the client to get out of the vehicle to assist us with turning (we suspect it's for fear of going over the edge!). Eventually we made it to the site. It was not enough to make Rodrigues happy that all the materials were there, including the precious water, which was stored in big, open-topped blue plastic drums. The problem was that no work was taking place, and Rodrigues gave vent to his disappointment. Lots of Haitian arm waving ensued, together with requests for extra *lajan* (money) for getting the materials up there.

It was then that I saw a 4-wheel drive truck approaching the site. The driver was frantically waving his arms and he appeared to be out of control of his vehicle. As this was a single track, he was heading straight for my Hyundai. Not wanting two accidents in one day, I hurriedly jumped into the driver's seat, started up, slammed into reverse and moved back no more than 5 feet, so that I could go off the track and into the jungle, thus avoiding the oncoming truck.

At this point over my shoulder I saw Rodrigues running towards me, followed by a hoard of arm-waving, angry Haitian workers. He jumped into the passenger seat and yelled, "Drive, get the fuck out of here!". This was just as the other truck passed me and came to a halt in a mound of sand. I could see in my rear-view mirror what the urgency was. When I reversed, I'd knocked over the plastic water butts! Water was sloshing everywhere! There would be no concrete poured that afternoon.

As I accelerated away from the site I could tell that Rodrigues was a little put out. I eased up on the throttle and ventured a tentative "Sorry about that". Rodrigues didn't respond. I started to wonder if he might lodge a complaint about me. His silence created an atmosphere and I felt uncomfortable. A few more minutes had passed when Rodrigues started shaking, his face contorted. Oh, shit! The words "fired before I'd really got started" were going through my brain. I thought he was going to rip into me with an almighty bollocking! I had messed up big time, so I braced myself for my rightly-deserved dressing down. Then out it came from the depths of his belly, a huge gust of laughter that he was unable to control. In-between bouts of gales of laughter, he recounted the water butts disaster. I couldn't contain myself either and joined in. As we reached Pétion-Ville we calmed down. Rodrigues exclaimed that it was the funniest thing that he had seen in years and that he needed a beer. I agreed, and steered directly to the Bar St. Pierre. Rodrigues refused to let me buy the beers. I did suggest going back to the office. "Office?", he laughed, "fuck the office!" he said, as he ordered two more Prestiges. The bières were placed in front of us. Rodrigues raised his glass. As he toasted, "Oh well, one more day behind schedule, this is Haiti!", I realised with glee that Rodrigues and I had bonded!

Chapter 27
LOCK DOWN

T he national presidential elections were held last Tuesday. The results were supposed to have been announced on Friday. Today is Tuesday February 14th, almost one week later, but no announcement so far. The "manifestations" started on Sunday, which coincided with Haiti's Kanaval preparations. Kanaval (Carnival) is a huge event which takes place the last weekend of February and it invariably turns violent! This is our third night of "lock down", that is to say that we and our clients have secured ourselves inside our residences. I have enough food to last me till the end of the week.

We have given shelter to Mitch and Ng, a couple of UN employees who were forced out of their vehicle at gunpoint. They had run to our gates where our security guard had let them in. We heard the explosion as their car was torched! We are also housing a local family who were burnt out of their house. There has been widespread rioting by supporters of Preval (the front runner in the election). They are demanding that he should be pronounced as president. UN troops have been generally ineffective, apart from an "action" near the airport, where they opened fire on armed rioters, killing an unconfirmed number. The Haitian Police (PNH) are nowhere to be seen on the streets (probably they've joined the rioters). The air has been thick with the smell of burning tyres. Barricades have been erected at critical points on the main roads, manned by armed mobs. Our house on Kenscoff Road is isolated, on either side of us are burning barricades.

From our vantage point on the roof we can see the mobs feeding the fires. There is plenty of fuel in the form of rubbish, tyres, trees, foliage and cars! Over the last two days team members have mounted various rescue missions. Some of our clients were housed at the Montana, which is the most prestigious hotel in the country (there is no star system here). The UN was based there to announce the election results, which made it a focus of attention for the mobs. The hotel was subsequently overrun by rioters. Our clients barricaded themselves in their rooms and had to be rescued by armed intervention from our team members. We were totally frustrated by being "locked down", with burning barricades preventing us from taking part in the action! The latest news is that 85,000 voting papers in favour of Preval have been found on a rubbish tip! This has enlivened the pro-Preval mobs. So, just when we thought the *manifestation* was running out of steam it is back on with renewed vigour! We managed to extract our UN guests and local family during a lull this afternoon.

Right now we are watching television, monitoring our radios with cell phones at the ready. E&E kits (escape & evasion) have been packed and we are ready to lay up in the jungle which surrounds our house, if need be. We don't think the mob will go very far into the jungle to look for us, because they are scared of Damballa, the Vodou serpent. Haiti is one of the few countries with no venomous snakes.

So, once more we sit and wait...

Chapter 28
I'VE GOT A BRAND NEW FRIGIDAIRE!

It has been relatively calm here since the chaos of the elections and the manic four days which were Kanaval (Carnival). I resigned from my job, then retracted! I am currently the hero of the moment. I decided to resign due to the leave rotations, i.e. seven days every six weeks. This would have meant four of my seven days flying to and from the UK, something totally impractical for me. On my exit interview the director general agreed with me and directed that our whole leave schedule be revised. I immediately got reinstated. After much discussion and many negotiations our terms of service have been substantially changed for the better. We now get eleven days leave every five weeks, on full pay! Good deal or what?

Mick, one of our team, was off duty in the Bucan bar. He was socialising with a group of UN personnel when he had an altercation with an off-duty UN cop. I don't know the details, but apparently Mick had pulled out his hand gun and threatened the UN cop. The next day our boss, Big Al, received a call from a local police contact. This resulted in Mike bundling up his gear and getting on the first flight to Miami! The UN cop had laid a complaint to the local PNH accusing Mick of "aggravated assault with a firearm", which meant that Mick would be arrested and tried before the courts, unless he paid 25,000USD to the poor UN cop for the distress he experienced! You really don't want to spend one second in a Haitian jail. So, the "fast exit plan" was implemented. The arrest warrant still stands, so Mick can't return to Haiti. The problem for me has been that I inherited his car! My original vehicle was a manual. I am a lazy driver. His car is an automatic and you really do need an automatic for the nature of the job that we do on the roads out here! I have been stopped a few times since by UN cops. Fortunately, I am able to prove my identity with my British passport, Haitian driving licence and Haitian identity card. Also luck has it that I look nothing like Mick, so his description doesn't fit me at all!

All of our usual duties continue. The airport runs are less exciting lately, as the UN and chimères have suspended hostilities. However a worrying trend has manifested itself in the last seven days. On the stretch of road which extends for about half a mile from Pan Américain to the Montana hotel, turning on Rue John Brown, there have been nine murders. All taking place at night, the victims being forced out of their vehicles, robbed and executed with a single gunshot to the base of the skull. Why it is especially worrying for us, is that all the victims were security personnel, except for one who was a Swiss national who worked as a teacher. All were dressed in the distinctive "uniform" of safari type vest and combat trousers, which is the current hallmark of the close protection industry worldwide. Suffice to say, I have stopped wearing my "safari" vest at night.

Since I have lived at my present address with three other guys a couple of us have been plagued by food thefts! One member of our household just feeds on what is available. He also likes to entertain Dominican Republic "ladies". The final straw came for me when I bought a litre of my favourite cranberry juice. I had one swig from it before going to bed. The next morning I found less than one inch in the bottom of the bottle! After some uncomfortable confrontations and all-round denials, there was only one course of action. So, I went into Pétion-Ville and bought myself a brand new refrigerator for 265USD, fully equipped with a built-in locking door! Haitians refer to all makes of refrigerators as "Fridgidares". It is strange but I am ecstatic about being the proud owner of my very own Fridgidare!

Chapter 29
TRANQUILLITY

W e have since received the pronouncement that Preval has been elected president, which has appeased the masses. The new president has called for calm, which will be enforced by his chimères, so we anticipate a period of relative tranquillity. As a show of good faith there have only been five kidnappings reported this week! The company has decided to have another "promotion", starting Monday! Our evacuated clients were returned to us this afternoon, so we picked them up from the airport for a return motorcade. I have a day off tomorrow so I will be rested, up and ready for next week's fray. I will be based at Martissant in Kafou. The markets opened this afternoon, so I have restocked my food supplies.

Chapter 30
TRANKIL, 'SPORTIF'?

Things are still quiet, apart from a UN action the other day on the airport road, when six more chimères were dispatched! The investiture of President Preval passed without too much incident, but having said that, there was a riot in the prison in Port-au-Prince which left an "undisclosed number dead". Apart from that, the streets have been as quiet as I have ever known them. There does appear to be a mood of optimism in the air, and a certain *trankil* (tranquillity). Last Wednesday night I took a group of our clients to the Pétion-Ville Club. It's the closest thing here to a country club. They had a good time because the clients were all South American and the club put on a set of Latino music from the Dominican Republic. It was impossible to stop them dancing! I returned them to the Montana Hotel afterwards and started heading up to Pétion-Ville to make my way home to Pelerin. I have mentioned before about the street people, the coco rats, beggars and urchins. As I had been driving out on my evening mission, I had passed one of the street girls who I now know to be named Teteh (pronounced titty!). Teteh had been in her usual spot on Rue Faubert, where she variously begs or plies her trade as a prostitute. She'd waved to me as I passed by, which she does to everyone.

It was approaching midnight when I turned into Rue Faubert after my Montana Hotel drop. My headlight was on full beam and I was able to make out Teteh being bent backwards over a low wall, her skirt pushed up around her waist, a hand clamped over her mouth. Her face was turned towards me. I could see that her eyes were wide with terror. The object of her dismay was a Haitian man who was straddling her, with his left hand clamped over her mouth and his right hand at her throat. His trousers had slipped to his knees and he was displaying an erection. I slowed down and drove up to them. The man retained his hand over Teteh's mouth and was shielding his eyes with his right hand. I got out of my car and started to walk towards them.

"Madame ou avec pwoblem?", I asked.

"Blan ou gardez mw sportif" (white man, you watch my sport), the man replied.

Given the circumstances my Kreyol deserted me. I yelled at him to leave her alone. He said "Ou gardez mw coopee bouzin bitch la" (you watch me fuck the whore). He started to make a thrusting motion with his hips. I just shouted at him to stop. Teteh was struggling and whimpering. I could see tears in her eyes.

I drew my gun, walked up to him and put the snout to his forehead. I was now screaming at him to get off, or I would fucking kill him. He understood that alright! I stepped back. He let go of her, stood up, pulled his trousers up and put away his rapidly-shrinking penis. All the time he was smirking at me and muttering in Kreyol. He backed away from me as I walked him down the road with my gun trained on him. He continued muttering and I could make out the odd word, but certainly understood "mouri" (dead). He made his right hand to simulate a gun pointed at me, pulled the imaginary trigger and said "mouri". He then disappeared down the road and I returned to Teteh. She was on her cell phone, gabbling away. Within seconds a posse of *bouzin*s arrived. They all gathered around her. One of the posse spoke English. She thanked me for protecting her friend, but also told me that I may have caused trouble for them and for myself, because the man who had attacked Teteh was an off-duty PNH cop from downtown Port-au-Prince. It is apparent that when off duty, some PNH tour Pétion-Ville to take part in what he had referred to as "sportif", that is the rape of prostitutes. Safe in the knowledge that the girls would or could not complain.

Teteh gathered herself together, gave me the customary Haitian kiss on each cheek, said "mesi mesyer" and gave me a hug. The other girls stood around and applauded. I got back into my car and drove off. I turned over in my head what someone had said to me some months before: "Haitians have short memories". I'm off on leave this weekend. I sure hope that he forgets before I get back.

Chapter 31
CONSENT?

I've been back one week after a much-needed holiday. Ironic that I had to travel 5,500 miles from the Caribbean to the Mediterranean to get a suntan! I was feeling a little apprehensive about going back out on the streets at night, after my last incident with Teteh and the off-duty cop. Whilst waiting at the departure gate at JFK airport, I saw a group of uniformed Chinese police and we got chatting. They spoke good English and I learned that they were bound for Haiti as part of the UN peacekeeping operation. I complimented them on their English-speaking skills. They were very proud that they had just completed an intense English course, designed to prepare them for their Haitian deployment. They seemed a little crestfallen when I advised them that the Haitian language was in fact Kreyol.

"But they do understand English, don't they?"

"Uhh, no", was my reply.

The Chinese cops dissolved into a group gabble in their native tongue. I left them to get on with it!

We now have a contingent of Peruvian UN troops on the streets of Pétion-Ville. I decided to approach an officer in charge of a patrol. He spoke reasonable English. I told him of the incident with the off-duty cop and the attempted rape. He assured me that it was UN policy to prevent abuse of women, whatever their status, and that nighttime patrols would be briefed to pay attention to the "street girls".

He must have been true to his word because each night that I have been out I have noticed that the troops appear to have enthusiastically thrown themselves into this aspect of their peacekeeping work. Each patrol has adopted a gaggle of girls!

Following that incident, I made some enquiries regarding the law covering rape. I ascertained that although in law it was a crime, in practice there is no such thing as consent in practical terms. In effect a man can have sex with a woman if he so desires. So the off-duty cop believed that it was his "right". The concept of "consent" does not seem generally to exist in Haitian culture. It may exist in law, but in practice women have been conditioned to accept sexual advances by men. Delving a little further, one night in the Bar St. Pierre I approached Mouse (Mirelle, one of the bar staff, known as Mouse because she is tiny).

"If someone stole your cell phone and you knew who the thief was, what would the police do about it?"

She looked at me puzzled, shrugged her shoulders and said, "Why would the police do anything? Maybe if you pay them something they might go with you to get your phone".

There has been an upsurge in violence. The post-election calm is starting to fall apart, with 21 murders, 28 kidnappings, and 7 policemen murdered in the Port-au-Prince area in the last week. The chimères are getting impatient with the new regime. It is rumoured that President Preval (RIP) has terminal prostate cancer and will not survive the year. The scene is being set to unleash the dogs of chaos!

Chapter 32
BEATINGS AND AN OVERDOSE!

P reval has failed to deliver. Shootings are up, kidnaps are up, robberies are up. The Brazilian UN troops have resumed their regular marksmanship practice most mornings on the airport road. It will be back to the pre-election levels soon! Nickson, the unofficial street parking/security man greets me with his usual patter:

"Everyday security, maximum security, I got good 'erb (cannabis). Give me 20USD", etc.

He also operates the workings of the half-dozen or so of his *bouzins* whose patch is the street outside the Bar St. Pierre. He sometimes adopts a Jamaican persona, other times US gangsta, but mainly street Haitian. He helped me out the other night when a Haitian reversed into my parked car, damaging the driver's door. He chased after him and gave him a beating, but didn't think to get his licence plate number! Well at least I could cover my back, when I submitted the accident report with an independent witness.

Nickson told me that after the incident with Teteh the local cops had been beating his "bitches". Apparently the girls were losing business by hanging around the UN troops as they were "shish" (Kreyol for tight fisted with their money!). Takings were down, so they had resumed their former pitches. The night shift cops had taken to patrolling around Pétion-Ville and whenever they spotted a *bouzin* they would give them a good slapping.

The "girls" had appealed to Nickson, so he approached the cops. The cops told him that they had received orders from downtown to do this. Money talks here so now, for the price of 100 gourdes or 5USD, the cops will flash their blue lights to signal their approach, giving the girls time to run and hide!

Last Sunday I was having a peaceful night in the Bar St. Pierre (everything happens within a radius of 200 metres from there). Nickson shouts out to me from the bar entrance (he is not allowed in).

"Mwe bitch malad" (one of my young lady friends is feeling unwell!).

No one in the bar moves. I look around, Nickson calls out again: "Mesyer Chris bitch malad".

I drain my Prestige and tell Mouse that I'll go and see what's up. On the ground outside is a young woman who Nickson refers to as Daphne. She is flat on her back with her feet in the open sewer that flows by. She appears to have vomited, judging by the stained bodice of her short purple velvet dress. Nickson is enquiring if she will be able to get back to work. Her friends are getting more hysterical.

There is no ambulance service here, so I go into my first aid routine: DRABC (Danger, Response, Airway, Breathing, Circulation).

"Check for danger", she is sufficiently far away from passing vehicles.

"Airway", I get down on my knees and tilt her head back, she makes an audible sucking noise on intake of breath.

"Breathing" is established.

"Circulation", I check for a radial pulse, nothing. Check for a carotid pulse, it's so faint I could barely detect it.

She was breathing and making guttural noises in her throat. I turned her into the recovery position. All the time I am speaking to her: "Daphne, Daphne, ou domi? ou malad? Allez". No response. I peel back her eyelids. Her eyes are unseeing, rolling back into her head. I ascertain that she has not had any alcohol and smell her breath to confirm. From my experience I guess that she has taken an overdose. I tell Nickson that she needs to go to the hospital. He tells me that he has to stay, to protect his "bitches" and pay the police. No one else is doing anything. I guess it's down to me!

I ask for help from her friends. A couple step forward, they have already made some money this evening, Mya and Sophia. I bring my car closer. We try to lift Daphne, she is a dead weight. Between us we lay her onto the back seat of my car and set off for the grandly-titled "Citi Hopital". If you are sick, the last place on earth that you want to go is to a Haitian hospital! The Citi Hopital is allegedly one of the better hospitals. There are no lights on, even though it's only about 2100 hours, and I have to wake the armed security guard to let us in. The interior is painted in that old, sick green colour. I am carrying the heavy end of Daphne. Her two friends have hold of her feet. She must weigh 15 stone! Her dress has ridden up and she doesn't appear to be wearing any panties! There is nowhere to put her, so we lay her down on the floor. I approach the bandit-proof screen with Mya and Sophia. They start gabbling to the disinterested clerk. They are talking fast and it's difficult for me to understand. What I do catch drift of is that before anything can happen, 500 gourdes has to be paid. There is silence, the girls look at the floor then look at me. Knowing what's coming, in resignation I pull out my wallet. The security guard and a helper start to drag Daphne off towards a dingy room. The guard's shotgun is slung around his shoulder as he bends down; it slides forward and smacks Daphne along the side of her head. She didn't flinch so must have been deeply unconscious. I go to assist. We lift her onto an examination couch. I go and sit on a stone bench in the waiting area.

After about half an hour, the two girls and a man dressed in green scrubs approached me. I am informed that Daphne has taken an overdose of what was probably aspirin and that 1000 gourdes is required for her treatment. I dutifully hand over the cash. I give Mya and Sophia a further 100 gourdes and tell them that I'm returning to the St. Pierre, and that 100 gourdes will cover the *tap tap* fare for the three of them to return to the bar. With my evening well and truly messed up, I have one more Prestige then return to my home.

A couple of nights later, I am driving by the Bar St. Pierre where I see the three girls. Daphne looks to be in fine health. I ascertained that she had accidentally taken too many tablets for her monthly abdominal pains. I tell her that she owes me 1600 gourdes and she offers to pay me "in kind", but I pass on that.

The Brazilian UN troops have resumed their regular marksmanship practice most mornings on the airport road.

Chapter 33

GUNFIRE, BEACH, CELLPHONE WARS

T he second Prestige had just slid down a treat. It was about 1900 hours. I was with Andy, my immediate boss. We were in the Bucan with an assorted group of UN cops and security people. Our radios crackle "Automatic gunfire Pelerin 9", which is where I live! Dan was at home and had called it in. Dan doesn't scare easily. The UN men hear the transmission. A general consensus is that we all go to investigate. Beers are swigged back! Bottles slammed down and we run to our vehicles. The big white UN Nissan patrol cars are parked immediately outside. I jump into Andy's Terracan. Five UN Nissan patrols set off in front of us, all with blue lights flashing and we fall in behind them.

As we pass the Pétion-Ville Commissariat on our way up the Kenscoff Road with the blue lights leading the way, I momentarily flash back to my police days in the UK. I am jolted out of my reverie not just by the rough roads but by the realisation that I was no longer a UK copper on the way to a Saturday night "punch up". We were responding to automatic gunfire in one of the most dangerous countries in the world after Iraq, rated alongside Somalia and Darfur by the US State Department. The alcohol instantly evaporated. We were on the job! The UN had decided on a show of force, and we were content to follow.

We arrived at Pelerin 9 to be met by Dan and our security guards. Me, Andy and the UN stand to, giving all-round cover. The guards tell us that a gunfight had broken out between two vehicles just outside the gates to our house, which had since sped off. The UN guys went looking for the cars involved. Me and Andy? We returned to the Bucan! The next day is Sunday and I am taking clients to the beach on the Cote d'Arcadiennes! No one else on the team wanted to do a "beach run". I was happy to give up my day off to have a day at the beach.

The route to Wahoo Bay is pretty tortuous, at one point fording a water hole, the brown water washing over the car's bonnet (that's the hood, for US readers!). We also encountered a couple of half-hearted local "checkpoints". That is, villagers on the route erecting barricades and trying to extort money from wealthy beach goers. I just bore down on them, forcing them to dive out of the way. To stop would mean rendering yourself vulnerable to robbery or kidnapping. The missionaries who stopped found this out to their cost.

We arrived at Wahoo, where the parking area was full of UN troop carriers. Our little party of four clients and I find ourselves a spot under a thatch shelter, right at the water's edge. We order langoustine fresh from the sea and what else but Prestige? On surveying the scene it appears that we are no longer in Haiti, but for today Wahoo has been transformed into the Copacabana! There were hundreds of off-duty Brazilian troops, all fit young men. Over the sound system boomed out Latino beats, no "Kompa" (Haitian pop music) today. The guys were everywhere, drinking and dancing samba. Unfortunately there were very few women, so they contented themselves with drinking and dancing.

Whenever a woman came into sight, hundreds of eyes followed her every move! It was Latino party time, all good natured, no fighting or loutish drunkenness. So after a relaxing day's duty on the beach, we returned home refreshed.

Our rival company is here. Their marketing campaign has been phenomenal! The whole of Pétion-Ville has been painted red by their advertising. They have really caught the locals' imagination. Their stores are now open and the crowds are besieging them. It is hard to navigate your way around the town due to the chaos. A slanging match has started due to the fact that our company had to pay $4 million to the Haitian government for the rights to operate. The rivals offered a mere $1 million for a licence and it was accepted. This has fuelled a war of words. The mud has started to fly. The next few months could prove interesting. Let the cell phone wars commence!

Chapter 34

LAND DISPUTES, QUICK DRAW AND FATAC

S aturdays are easy days. Late start, early finish and dressed down, as our clients wear shorts and flip flops. We can wear jeans if we wish. I had just dropped off my clients and I was tucking into my French toast and café au lait at the Villa Créole. I had finished eating and already downed my third powerful Haitian Rebo coffee when my radio burst into life.

On a Saturday?

It was Pierre, who was on duty at the Main Switch Control (MSC) installation at Canapé Vert.

"I have a mob of about 100 with machetes, rocks and handguns chanting that this was their land and that it had been stolen from them."

I pay up, jump into my Terracan, and I am heading towards him. From the radio transmissions it was clear that I was the nearest unit. It is agreed that I should "approach with caution, assess the situation and report back".

Pierre has the MSC "locked down". "The mob is getting rowdy", was his last report. I start climbing the hill towards the front gates. I have my windows down and I can hear the chanting.

As I round the bend I see the tail end of the mob jog trotting off up a track which surrounds the MSC.

I see men brandishing handguns and others carrying machetes wrapped in white cloth. I know that white is associated with death and white cloth headscarfs are a Vodou symbol.

I hang back until the mob has moved out of sight before I move up to the front gates which are 20 feet high, as is the wall which surrounds and encloses the MSC.

The guards quickly let me in. I report back to control that I am on site. I relay my message that the MSC is safe and that there has been no breach of the perimeter wall. Pierre is inside the main building maintaining its integrity.

I start an internal foot patrol of the perimeter. There are vantage points where I can view the mob.

It appears that as the mob progresses along the wall, being unable to find a way in, they become even more angry. This is manifested by the sporadic gunfire which breaks out, the unwrapped machetes being waved in the air and the white linen now worn as head scarfs! All this riotous activity is hard work in the hot sun and eventually when they can see that there is no way that they can gain access, the mob breaks up as interest fades.

I receive a phone call. Apparently, there is indeed a dispute over the ownership of the land, but it was supposed to have been resolved four years ago. Why has it been rekindled? Could it be the arrival of our competitors? The "war of words" and the sniping has intensified.

A few days later I was off duty, driving down to the traffic lights by the Tiger Market. The lights were green and there was a

Prado stationary at the lights, with a man leaning against the driver's door, chatting to the driver. I pull up directly behind the Prado and wait for a while. The lights turn red. The lights turn green again but the chatting continues. I honk my horn and the chatting still continues. I call out "Mesyer ou bloque, avancee sil vou plait".

The man in the road who is chatting with the driver casually turns his head, looks at me and in a disdainful manner makes a sucking sound with his tongue, pressing the back of his teeth, then returns to his chatting. In doing this, he turns his right hip in an exaggerated manner, so that he makes it clear for me to see the outline of a handgun under his shirt. I call out to the PNH cop who is on duty at the intersection. He motions back to me that I should get out of my car and talk to the man.

I exit my vehicle and I am about 10 feet away from him when he turns towards me. His right hand is edging towards his gun and he fumbles to lift his shirt. The next thing I know is that I have drawn my handgun, I am in combat stance with the two-handed grip and I am pointing it at his head. He now has his gun held limply in his right hand, pointing to the ground.

I shout "tonbe ou zamm" (drop your gun).

He looks to his right.

In my peripheral vision, I see the cop advancing towards me with his rifle trained on me. He is shouting "Anba ou zamm" (lower your gun).

The man tucks his gun back into his jeans. The Prado has sped off!

I slowly lower my gun, the cop is in front of me pointing his rifle at my head. I holster my weapon and raise my hands.

The man is now sniggering and muttering to the cop. The cop tells him to shut up. The cop demands to see my gun permit, which I keep in an ID holder that I wear around my neck. His rifle is still on me, I produce my permit and he lowers his rifle to examine it. He is satisfied with that and my Haitian NIC card (national identity card).

He then delivers what I perceive to be a "bollocking" to the man, who slinks off chastened. He turns to me and gabbles on in Kreyol. I can make out enough to understand that I have committed a criminal act and I should face a court. Or I can accept an on-the-spot fine and escape a conviction! I hand over the contents of my wallet - 1000 Haitian gourdes (about 13USD, I keep the rest of my cash zipped inside a belt with a money compartment). We shake hands; he has made the equivalent of a week's pay, and I still have an unblemished character.

Where I live, at Pelerin 9 on Rue Kenscoff, is a dangerous stretch of road. It is littered with disabled, broken-down vehicles, and road traffic accidents are a regular feature. On both Saturday and Sunday this week I have seen bodies in the road, the victims of fatal RTA's (Road Traffic Accidents) or FATACS (Fatal Accidents), as we used to refer to them when I was a copper in England.

On Monday I was driving down Rue Kenscoff on my way to my night shift. I was giving Yolen our housekeeper a lift, as she lives in Pétion-Ville. We had only got to Pelerin 7 when we met traffic gridlock, nothing moving. So we sat and waited. Yolen speaks reasonable English. She enquired of some passing pedestrians as to what the problem was. Apparently, an accident had occurred involving a motorbike and a car, and the motorcyclist was dead. The traffic starts to move slowly. Eventually we reach the site of the FATAC. The body is still in the road and a *tap tap* is parked close by. The *tap tap* driver is deciding whether or not to take the body. As I have pointed out before, there is no ambulance service in Haiti. The sticking point for him to take the body is who will pay for his fare? No one is willing to foot the bill! Yolen tells me if no family or friends are available then the body will just stay there.

I call the *tap tap* driver over and give him 25 gourdes. With the help of other *tap tap* passengers, the body is loaded onto the flatbed of the vehicle and shoved between the two rows of passengers with the head hanging out the back and the lifeless eyes staring up to the sky. No one seems concerned; the passengers ignore the body. The driver continues at his usual speed. The head is bouncing around, spilling blood and grey "mush" onto the road. I ask Yolen where he will take the body. She tells me that they will put it out in Pétion-Ville, where a UN Patrol will find it and take it away. I ask her what would have happened before the UN. She advised me that unless the family dealt with it then it would just stay where it was until animals ate it or someone dumped it somewhere out of the way.

Again, there is no ambulance service in Haiti, and little charity.

Chapter 35

RANDOM ACTS OF VIOLENCE

A few days later, having completed my morning client drop-offs, I was feeling thirsty and decided to buy a cold drink from the shop at the National petrol station, situated on Rue Delmas. As I pulled onto the forecourt there were a couple of vehicles parked at the fuel pumps, with the drivers engaged in refuelling their cars. I parked away from the fuel pumps, got out of my vehicle, locked it and started walking towards the shop. After a few paces I heard a commotion coming from inside the shop. A man came running out, closely pursued by the station security guard, who I knew. The security guard was brandishing his short-barrelled, pump-action shotgun. He called out to the running man, who was heading to my left and wide of me. I saw that he had a handgun in his right hand.

Instantly I knew what was about to happen. I dropped to my right knee, drawing my Glock as I did. At that moment I heard the blast from the shotgun. The running man fell flat on his face on the ground right in front of me, having been shot in the back. I remained on my right knee with my gun trained on the apparently dead man. The security guard ran up to the body and called to me, "Pagen pwoblem, gason mouri, anba ou zam" (no problem, man is dead, lower your gun). I lowered my gun and stood up. I saw the gaping, bloody wound in the centre of the man's back. The security guard confiscated the dead man's gun. He told me that the man was a "vagabon" had tried to hold up the shop. The guard

137

further told me that he would contact the UN to remove the body. I holstered my gun, went into the shop and bought my drink. When I came out of the shop, it was business as usual; cars were manoeuvring around the body; people were walking past to pay for their fuel, paying scant attention to the bloody dead body.

That is Haiti.

Chapter 36
U.D.A. MAN IN HAITI!

T
He rival cell phone company had quickly established themselves in Haiti. As we were in the same business it was not unusual to bump into them on our travels around Pétion-Ville. They had their own contracted security team. If we were travelling with clients and we encountered a rival executive and their security entourage, we exchanged discrete nods. It was a professional etiquette that was unspoken but mutually agreed on. As there were a limited number of top class, relatively safe restaurants in Pétion-Ville, it was inevitable that the senior executives of both companies would find themselves double-booked! There was no open hostility as such but being seated at adjoining tables was not on. Before tables were booked, we as security would send an "advance" to the chosen restaurant to check it out and receive the diners. As well as doing a security sweep, we would check with the head waiter whether our rivals were also booked in on that day, and if they were, could we be seated a suitable distance from them? Sometimes it was necessary to negotiate a rearranging of tables! Once our clients were safely seated, we would mount a discrete guard, both inside and outside of the venue. One man would be detailed to stay outside with the vehicles, ready for a fast extraction.

We always managed to acquire a decent meal on these jobs. Quite often our vehicles would be parked right next to those of the rival team. It was inevitable that we would end up chatting with their security. Whenever I was on outside duty, it seemed that it would always be the same rival security man on duty with me. Inevitably we would get talking, and he turned out to be quite friendly and engaging. We agreed on everything about living and working in Haiti. I assumed from his accent that his background was military or the Royal Ulster Constabulary. It was during our third meeting that he told me that he was a loyalist and that his "military" experience had been gained in the Ulster Defence Association, a prescribed paramilitary terrorist organisation since 1992! He was an interesting character and was totally at ease with my police and military reserve history. He went so far as to tell me that with the skills that he had learnt, it meant him either ending up doing this, or becoming a gangster!

Chapter 37
JACMEL JAIL

Well I suppose that if you're going to be locked up in jail in Haiti, then the *commissariat (police station)* in Jacmel has got to be the best of only bad options. Things have been going better for me over the last few weeks. I had suffered a slight psychological dip around my first anniversary here. Then I ran the security at the "Musique en Folie" event at the *Musée de la Canne à Sucre (sugar cane museum)*, which proved to be a huge success, with crowds of 30,000 plus enjoying themselves. I even managed to have my photo taken with "Non-m-Sa" (a sister duet Kompa band). They are big in French Guiana!

The magistraterial elections have been going on countrywide, Pétion-Ville being a battlefield most nights, with clashes between opposing politically-sponsored *raras (horn and drum musical processions)*. The actual elections took place last Sunday, with amazingly only three murders committed at polling stations!

How did I come to spend four hours in custody in Jacmel?

I have secured my position as event security manager after my previous success in designing out problems at other events, i.e. the siting of the kiosk and distribution of freebies. Before I took charge, these things just happened without any regard of the consequences and riots ensued. You may recall at the last Musique en Folie, when promotional staff were having T-shirts ripped from their backs. Last week Jacmel hosted the Wyclef Jean Film Festival. Wyclef is a world-renowned musician of this era originating from Haiti. The town of Jacmel is a two-hour drive through notorious Kafou and over the mountains. It's probably as good as it's possible to get in Haiti.

We set off; Madame Russo, the marketing director and Mesyer Firdi, the events manager and I, plus two local security guards in a follow car. It should have been an omen for me when my car broke down in the middle of Kafou and we had to do an "under arms" vehicle switch! We arrived in Jacmel and found our accommodation at Indian Rocks Dive Centre, owned and run by Mesyer Gilbert Assad (pronounced Jill bear). Gilbert turned out to be quite a colourful character; when I asked him about his business, he rolled up his shirt sleeve to reveal a tattoo of a pirate! He regaled us with tales of embargo-breaking runs between Florida and Cuba, with whiskey and diesel smuggling being his main occupation! He insisted that he was a man of morals; no people, guns or *cockayeen (cocaine)*. "I have my own political party. I stood at the last elections", he announced, "my party is Baton, Mackaka, Ti tanyen". He explained that the party title meant that if you are bad we beat you with a small stick, if you continue bad we use a big stick and if that doesn't work we bury you in the mass graves off Route Nacional 1!

The event was going fine, developing into a success. On Friday afternoon I escorted Madame Russo to the press conference in the town hall. We had just returned to our accommodation when I got a phone call from Firdi, telling me that his two marketing boys had been beaten up, arrested and were in jail! Madame Russo, Gilbert and I set off to the commissariat. On the way, Gilbert tells us not to worry as he is friends with the commissar (local chief of police). Outside the commissariat is traffic chaos, so I drop off Madame Russo and Gilbert and go and park the car. I arrive back on foot about ten minutes later to see an agitated Madame Russo in a heated Kreyol conversation with Gilbert! Gilbert tells me that she has become the problem and to get rid of her and return myself. I convey Madame Russo to the festival site. She is fuming over what she sees as an abuse of power by the police. I returned to the cop shop, where Gilbert tells me that Madame Russo had been ranting and raving, demanding that the chief of police be brought before her, and shouting that she was going to close the event, unless her boys were released.

I got the story from Gilbert. The undisputed facts were that the two marketing boys had found themselves with a surplus of freebee T-shirts, so using their initiative, whilst we were at the press conference, they drove on to the beach to distribute the shirts. A policeman stopped them and told them no vehicles were allowed past that point on the beach. What is not clear is why a "manifestation" then developed. My guess is that they argued with the police, causing a crowd to gather. The crowd see the T-shirts and tried to steal them, which caused a melee. In this melee a car door was slammed shut, trapping a policeman's little finger! This gave the police the green light to act tough. They then proceeded to rough up and arrest our boys. Gilbert assured me that he could still negotiate their release after the negative start caused by Madame Russo. We entered the police station where there were six SWAT (Special Weapons And Tactics) officers, variously lounging around drinking beer and Guiness, all armed with assault rifles. As we entered, the SWAT team gathered themselves up and surrounded us with rifles at the low port.

I introduced myself. Before I could say much more I was shepherded towards an open gate and I found myself in a holding cell. The gate was slammed shut and the lock turned. Gilbert said "Don't worry, ou garunti, assurance". In other words, I was being held hostage! I inspected my cell, which was about twenty feet square with a concrete floor, central drain, light blue walls to about four feet then white up to the ceiling, with a dim 60 watt bulb hanging from a flex in the centre. Surprisingly it didn't smell too bad. I was the sole occupant. I sat on the concrete bench and contemplated my fate. I had been taken hostage. They believed that I had cash and might be prepared to make a "donation" to get us all released. They hadn't searched me, so I still had my gun!

It was now about 2000 hours. There was nothing that I could do. My fate was in the hands of others. To pass the time I sat in a yogic pose, breathed deeply and tried to clear my mind. At 2345 hours, Gilbert spoke to me through the bars of the gate.

"Go with this officer and buy 'something special' for the commissar."

"What do you mean?"

"You will see."

Gilbert disappears.

The cop unlocks the gate, draws his hand gun and marches me at gunpoint to the *boutik* next to the commissariat. I am wondering, what the hell can I buy the commissar that will be special? As I stand at the entrance to the shop I can't help but chuckle to myself as I see the shelves stacked with "something special" whiskey! So 5000 gourdes later, and two bottles of "something special" in a black plastic bag, I am returned to the cop shop to find our two boys receiving their property back. I ascertain that there will be no charges or court appearances and that we are free to go. Gilbert tells me that we must go to the festival to see the commissar. We push through the crowds to the VIP area to find a gaggle of uniformed police, prostitutes and other business types sitting around a table. I am introduced to much hand shaking and cheek kissing (females, that is!). Gilbert gives me a nudge so I profer the black bag, which is greeted with a roar of approval. The party kicks off to the sounds of Wycleff.

Wyclef Jean Film Festival

Chapter 38

TERMINATION

I t has been an unsettling few weeks. Everyone on the team has been served with notice of termination as of February 28th, 2007. Apparently we are an "expensive commodity" and are to be cut and replaced by cheaper models.

The Christmas period had its usual chaotic climax, with the chimères being interviewed on radio and offering special, discounted Christmas kidnapping deals of 4,500USD. What a bargain! The serious side of this has been the targeting of children for kidnapping. Recent kidnap attempts had failed due to the victims having the audacity to fight back, dispatching some of the aggressors to join the spirit world. In an attempt to reinforce their ruthless image, the gutless bastards have not only snatched a bus load of school girls but also raided a girls' school, taking six young girls. The worst incident by far, though, was the taking of two teenage twin sisters a few months before. You may remember how that ended!

The company has been increasing its coverage, which has meant the construction of antennae in more and more dangerous places, where the UN and police do not patrol. I have accompanied technicians to some of these sites, where I have had to negotiate with the local gangs, inevitably having to dispense *"kob" (cash)* to the leaders, to ensure our access and safe passage. We are also being called to take on more responsibilities. We now have to escort our local dealers into the slums of Port-au-Prince on enforcement operations, clamping down on unauthorised dealerships. Of course, these dealerships are not run by the most scrupulous of people, who have not been best pleased by our disruption of their illegal activities. It has been necessary for me to make more than one extraction under fire during the last week! Bearing this in mind, the company still wants to replace us with cheaper alternatives, people who have no local knowledge or built up experience of Haiti.

A couple of weeks ago I was on an airport run. Whilst waiting for the client to exit the airport at arrivals, I got chatting with a "red cap" (airport baggage porter). He explained to me that they are self-employed and exist on the tips they receive from bag carrying. Therefore, if a traveller's bag falls from a trolley, which is inevitable due to the uneven floor, then it is fair game for the red caps to pounce on it and basically hold the traveller's bag to ransom, whilst scuttling out of the airport and waiting for the owner to find them, reclaiming their bags but at a price.

As we chatted, the strains of "Oh Happy Days" drifted out of the interior of the exit hall. I could see that inside was a gospel choir who were advancing to the exit. They were shuffle dancing, hand clapping and singing, wearing purple and gold edged robes. As they emerged from the exit into the light, they continued singing, clapping and swaying in time to the song. Opposite them were the waiting crowds, under the green and white striped canopy. Dutifully the throng under the canopy joined in. The whole place was a joyous singing, clapping, swaying outpouring of Christian love.

Pasteur Louis stepped forward with an interpreter, and in time with the rhythm of the song he told the people that this was the first visit of his church to his brothers and sisters in Haiti. He explained how he would be giving away bibles and T-shirts, but most of all he would be giving them the word of the Lord. I saw an assistant dragging a couple of large, laundry-type bags, which were bursting at the seams with purple and gold T-shirts! It must have been at the same time that I saw the bags that the interpreter passed on the information to the crowd that Pasteur Louis was "giving". With that, the crowd swarmed over the five-feet-high railings under the canopy. You don't stand in the way of a mob of Haitians and a freebie! The choir was mobbed! Oh Happy Days was transformed into shrieks and shouting.

The swaying and dancing turned into pushing and shoving. T-shirts seemed to be flying out of the bags! Choristers were knocked off their feet, Pasteur Louis was appealing and pleading, crying "Easy chil'ren". The airport cops, never ones to miss an opportunity for baton practice, waded in. No discrimination here! Choristers and locals each getting an equal portion of baton! The cops let off some CS gas for good measure, and people were running in all directions. The "red caps" must have developed an immunity to the CS, because they were grabbing abandoned bags as fast as they could. I motioned to Pasteur Louis for him and his choir to follow me upwind of the gas clouds. I guess he must have wanted to stay with his people's suffering, as I unfortunately lost sight of him as I ran away from the CS.

Event Security Manager

Chapter 39

CALL SIGN CHOPPER ALL AT SEA!

I was one of the terminated. No reason given. Just "Thank you, but no thank you". However I was aware that I had not endeared myself to some of the other team members. My appointment to the position of events security manager had ruffled some feathers. A team meeting had been called to formulate a plan to prevent the merchandising stalls at upcoming events from being ransacked by over-enthusiastic music fans. In the past, staff had been injured and large-scale theft of cell phones and goods had occurred. The general consensus was that "more guns" would solve it. I disagreed. Those who opposed me suggested that I should attend the next event and show them how it should be done. I had a very good idea what the problem was and how I could solve it, based on my experience of music festivals in the UK. I happily accepted the challenge and added that I would do it alone.

Comments such as "smart ass" and "who the fuck does he think he is?" followed me as I left the room.

The regular promotional open-air music festival was due to take place the following Saturday afternoon. I arrived on the site as the stage was being erected and the event manager was present. I asked him what had happened on previous occasions. He updated me and I then asked him where the merchandise canopy and stalls were to be located. He showed me the markings in the dirt where it was to be set up. In this position it would be free-standing, with no all-round physical protection. The event manager confirmed what I suspected, which was that as the fans became more excited they had invaded the stalls from all sides, and the staff had become overrun, resulting not only in injuries being suffered but also in substantial amounts of merchandise and cell phones being stolen. The manager went on to say that it had been decided to place it there so that the staff and customers had a view of the stage.

I knew immediately what had to be done. Only one side needed to be open to serve the customers. The other three sides required protection. By now, a number of large cargo vans had arrived on the site. I spoke to the drivers and ascertained that some of the vehicles would be staying for the duration of the show. The promotions team arrived. I supervised their placing of the canopy and stalls. I then, with the inducement of 25 gourdes each, persuaded the drivers of three cargo vans to park as tightly as they could around the three sides of the canopy and stalls, leaving one side open and facing the stage. To further secure the canopy, we pulled two of the stalls across the front, leaving a narrow entrance. The manager and I positioned ourselves at the front entrance to "meet and greet" customers. We also deployed the young promotional staff in front of us, as an extra barrier to give-away freebies which would deter the less serious customers. As an added ring of security, other traders had spontaneously set up beside our protective vans. I was confident that we could do no more to secure our assets. Suffice to say, the event went off without a hitch. None of our staff were injured and nothing was stolen. Excellent sales figures ensued and the event organisers were of course delighted.

Subsequently the event manager had sung my praises, confirming my position as events security manager. This had obviously irked some of my teammates. My good friend Corwin suddenly decided to resign. He told me that he was moving to the Dominican Republic to start a new life. I had a sinking feeling that my time was up, and I was right. Oh well, one door closes, another door opens. Again putting Haiti behind me.

Thank you for the amazing experiences. I will never forget you.

Chapter 40
A LIFE ON THE OCEAN WAVES

A new chapter was opening up for me and I knew where I was going. During my last few months in Haiti I had been receiving emails and the odd phone call from the maritime security company in Devonshire, England that I had previously worked for, on the US Mediterranean Prepositioning Fleet. They had secured contracts with various shipping lines to provide security for ships sailing around the Horn of Africa. The activities of the Somalian pirates had become more and more daring, brazen and vicious.

I had worked all of my adult life to be where I was now. Our kids had grown up and flown the nest. I was in a good financial position. In my terms, I had made it. I had taken some huge risks, been under fire, faced and seen death on a number of occasions. It was so relaxing to know that now my life was together and I could take things easy going forward, because that was what you were supposed to do when you were 57 years of age, wasn't it? I was heading towards my 60's and retirement. Life was good. Or was it? Yes it was, but my spirit was still restless. One last big job? I needed to do something. I wasn't ready to fade into oblivion. "Never let your memories" crept back into my consciousness. Frances and I were sitting watching the television news report of another ship having been taken by Somali pirates. I looked at her and she looked at me. No words were exchanged. The answer to my restlessness was staring me in the face.

"I know what's coming next!", retorts Frances.

I shrug my shoulders.

"I need to do something", is my reply.

We both knew then that I would soon be leaving on my next chapter of adventures. Within a couple of days I received a call from the maritime company, offering me anti-piracy work as either a team leader or team member.

Back home and comfortably settled into my new home on the waterfront looking out onto the Severn Estuary. It was summertime. I loved sitting gazing out to sea, watching the sun rise as the ships sailed in and out of the Royal Portbury Dock. The Grimaldi lines, NYK, UECC, Wallenius Wilhelmsen, to name but a few of the car carriers bringing vehicles from the Far East to our shores.

Meanwhile, on the other side of the planet, Somalian pirates were hitting the headlines with their daring attacks which were growing in audacity. Human and shipping hostages were being taken at will from a slow-to-respond maritime industry. Companies were popping up and recruiting retired military men for seaborne operations. I had previously worked for a well-established and respected UK maritime security company, both before and in between my Haiti and Iraq adventures.

And so it began. Most of my deployments were short, from 10 days to two weeks in duration. Often I would return from a ten-day trip, be home for maybe two, three days to a week and then be gone again.

Chapter 41
SALTY OLD SEA DOG

I regularly went on anti-piracy missions. Most were short trips, anything from eight to fourteen days. The majority of the jobs were on car carriers which had thirty metre freeboards. In the early days these jobs were unarmed. The only advantage of this was that it forced us to be inventive in our methods of protection. We always scoured the ship for scrap metal, which we could use to throw at any assailants. On one voyage we made replica rifles from steel tubes and wood. However the most frequently suggested improvised weapon was the petrol bomb. Having trained with petrol bombs in riot training in the police, I knew how unreliable they could be. For a start, I knew that in order to be effective, the bottles obviously needed to smash in order to ignite, therefore a hard surface for them to impact upon was required. New team members would be convinced that petrol bombs were the complete solution and insisted that they would work.

I remember well the first occasion when a team member would not listen and was adamant that the petrol bomb was the answer to our problem. He was itching to prove me wrong. His opportunity came one morning when we had been tailed by a skiff with the standard issue of five crew. We had shouted and thrown scrap metal at them but they were persistent and wouldn't take our advice or our hint. Oddly they had not produced any weapons so far. I could see that Rick was almost beside himself, virtually begging me to give him permission to throw his bomb. I must admit that I was getting rather annoyed. This skiff required a show of force. I was just about to give Rick the "go", when one of the skiff's crew pulled back a canvas cover and started to pick up an AK. That confirmed it! The word "go" had barely left my lips when Rick had lit the bomb's taper and hurled it directly at the skiff. We watched expectantly; the trajectory was perfect, on target. His aim was good and true. The bomb however, simply hit the wooden hull of the skiff, bounced up in the air, plopped into the water and was immediately extinguished. Undeterred, before we knew it Rick had his next bomb lit up in the air and again bang on target. Unfortunately the bomb landed on some rolled-up canvas on the deck of the skiff and failed to break. One of the pirates instinctively picked it up and threw it back at us. It smashed against the steel stern of our ship where the petrol ignited, the flames cascading harmlessly down into the sea. The pirates fired a few bursts of automatic AK at us but their aim was wildly off, as they were bouncing around in our wake and merely wasting ammo. We took cover nonetheless. In between bursts we smashed a few more petrol bombs against our stern so that a sheet of flames rained down. Mercifully the pirates dropped back, letting off a couple more bursts of bravado fire before skimming off in search of their next victim. "Tea and debrief on deck", I shout. With brews in hand whilst still maintaining watch we have a hot debrief. Rick feels justified in the effectiveness of petrol bombs. I can't disagree with the ultimate effectiveness of cascading fire down onto the heads of any attackers, but I insist that there has to be a better way of delivering fire to any future aggressors. I apologise to the bosun for the scorch marks to the stern of his beloved ship and promise him that I will come up with a better way to protect the ship which doesn't involve burning the paint!

I put some thought as to the best way to repel any future attackers. I studied the modus operandi of previous attacks. It was virtually always their tactic to approach the stern of the car carriers, because the structure of the underside of the ramp (the part which was lowered to the dock side, to allow the cars to be loaded or unloaded) had bracing bars across them, which presented as a ladder for the pirates to climb up and board the ship. We tried various methods of raining burning petrol down onto any potential attackers. Whichever method we tried, meant scorching the paintwork and upsetting the bosun! So, pouring petrol down the superstructure of the stern and smashing petrol bombs was out. In any case, the flames would fall into the water close to the stern. The skiffs could easily stand off a few feet and remain safe, out of reach of the flames.

Ships are constantly being repainted, which means that there are plenty of empty paint tins lying around. Paint thinners, along with petrol, were readily available. The plan that I came up with was to half fill empty paint tins with petrol or paint thinners. I acquired an emergency distress flare from the ship's stores, along with a pair of leather protective gauntlets. The plan was that upon a pirate encounter we would show ourselves, which we did as per our SOP's (Standard Operating Procedures) at the time. From cover with minimal exposure, we would throw the paint can of petrol at the skiff, hopefully showering the occupants in fuel. They should realise what they were covered in and what our likely next action might be, causing them to give up their attempt. However should this not deter them, then the "TL" (team leader), wearing protective gauntlets, would brandish the flare and shout out warnings, notwithstanding that the instructions were not likely to be understood. If the pirates, who were now doused in fuel, continued to pursue the ship then the "TL" was to hold the flare above his head, ignite it and throw it at the fuel-splashed skiff. The team liked it, but would it work?

We didn't have long to wait in order to find out, as the very next day we were probed! This wasn't unusual as in those days it was a daily occurrence before the International Recommended Transit Corridor (IRTC) and coalition naval forces patrolled the seas. Suffice to say my defence system worked. The farthest I ever got into raining down fire was holding the flare aloft and threatening a fiery death.

So commenced my five-year adventure in anti-piracy, when piracy attacks were at their height. Within weeks of touching down back in the UK, I was off again on unarmed anti-piracy jobs. I was the team leader. This was all new and we made it up as we went along. I have no memory of the name of the ship or anything else really, apart from the fact that the ship had a low freeboard, we were unarmed and that I was team leader. We were unarmed as in no guns, because at this stage it was risk assessed by the company as not necessary. We had scoured the decks and the bosun's locker for scrap metal which we could use to throw at any potential boarders. At each stand to position we had stockpiled odd bits of metal, ready to be thrown.

After a few days we were in the Indian Ocean approaching the island of Socotra, a pirate stronghold. Through binoculars it was plain to see the skiffs on the beach. Knowing the impending possibility of a piracy probe, I had called the team to stand to positions. The crew were in lockdown. Ahead I could see a skiff, just sitting there waiting. There were no other ships in front of us but there was a Turkish ship following some miles behind. These were the early days, there was no international organisation to combat piracy. No "standard operating procedure". It was down to the team leader to deal with whatever confronted him. As we drew level with the skiff I could see what looked like five fishermen on board. They waved empty plastic water bottles, calling out for refills I presumed. We ignored them. As we passed by the skiff I walked towards the stern, level with them. As I reached the stern I saw that the skiff's outboard motor had burst into life. I was alone on the stern. The freeboard was at a height of about twenty feet above the water. The skiff skimmed the waves and positioned itself directly behind the ship, bouncing around in our wake. I gripped the hand rail and glowered at them. They put their empty water bottles down and pulled back a cover to reveal their stash of AK-47 assault rifles. Each one of the former "fishermen" is now brandishing an AK and making it ready. I'm receiving radio messages asking what's happening.

"Radio silence, wait out", I reply.

The pirates obviously realise that I'm not alone but are not sure of the nature of the backup that I have. They appear to be reasonably disciplined, as they cock their weapons almost in time. The sun is bearing down on my head and shoulders. The wind is gently whistling, the ship's engine is thrumming away. I don't know why, but I shout out to them in Kreyol.

"Ou mem chef la?". I quickly add in English "Bossman?".

A tall, ugly bastard, wearing a red and white shemagh, stands up in the helm, flanked by his gun-toting crew of four. He beats his chest and shouts back "Chief". I eye him up. He is older, the other four are his boys. He is in charge. "Americans", he sneers. He then makes a theatrical nasal snort and derisively gobs a thick green mucus into the foaming water in front of him. I study his face, snort hard and spit straight into the sea just in front of the skiff. In response to his challenge I snarl back "Americans no, British!", I shout as I vigorously jab my chest with the forefinger of my right fist. I then growl the immortal internationally understood two words, "Fuck off!". Much to my surprise, ugly bastard replies in English. "British, British, ah you train me coast guard, we don't take you". With that the skiff turns and speeds off. I heave a bewildered sigh of relief. I feel the tension seep out of me. I sent a radio transmission to stand down.

The replies come back: "How the fuck did you do that?".

"My natural charm" I reply, "get me a brew someone". About an hour later I'm up on the bridge with the captain and chief mate quaffing tea and going over the sequence of events of the encounter, so that the captain can send a report to his head office. The ship's radio bursts into life. The international language of the sea is English. A heavily-accented voice immediately grabs our attention as its sense of terror is conveyed to us. It is the captain of the Turkish ship that was following us about fifteen miles away. He is pleading for help as pirates are attempting to board his ship. We listen in silence. The radio messages become more frantic, then quiet, an eerie quiet. The ship had been taken.

Chapter 42
ZIMBABWE

It was late summer 2007. Between anti-piracy deployments I took on odd security jobs, which was how I found myself working at a music festival at Powderham Castle, Exeter. The beneficiary of the event was a charity called Eco Dome. I was fascinated by the Eco Dome structures, which were made from recycled plastic tubing rammed with earth, coiled to form a dome shape, then hand plastered, adobe style, with a mud and cement mixture! These buildings could be quickly built to afford viable housing, especially in poorer countries. They were certificated to withstand earthquakes to California standards. I was intrigued by these domes and the humanitarian application for them in post-disaster environments, or in countries where the infrastructure was poor and there were no regulations for home building. I was pleasantly surprised to find out that the UK base for the charity was in Cardiff, Wales. This was roughly a 40-minute drive from my home in Portishead near Bristol, England. I was keen to find out more about the whole Eco Dome project. So within a week I had made an appointment to visit the charity offices. I duly attended the office where I was welcomed and advised that the CalEarth Eco Dome institute was in Hesperia, a city located in California, in the Mojave Desert and that maybe next year they could send me on a training course there. I came away enthused but frustrated in equal portions. I desperately wanted to learn how to build the domes but couldn't wait a year to do it. I suffer from terminal impatience, so I counted up my American Airline points from my trips to and from Haiti. I had hundreds of thousands, in fact, enough for a number of transatlantic flights! I self-funded the cost of my course. In double-quick time I was booked to fly to Los Angeles, then on to Hesperia and the CalEarth Institute. I arrived at the institute and set up my two-man tent, which was to be my accommodation for the duration of the week-long course.

I enjoyed all aspects of the training, from the lectures given by Nader Khalili, the Iranian-born architect of the structures and the founder of the institute, to the actual hard physical labour required to build them. Khalili was a charismatic mentor who used the poems of Rumi, a 13th-century Sufi mystic, to illustrate his principles of dome building.

The other students were drawn from all over the United States, so I was the lone Brit foreigner. Most were young, idealistic student types, nothing like my former American coworkers! None were of my age or background. Notwithstanding this, we all got on really well due to our enthusiasm to become dome builders. The days were ten hours long, of mostly physical work. Evenings consisted of communal meals and early to bed.

One evening I decided to take the institute mountain bike to ride into Hesperia for dinner. I noticed a sushi restaurant. I had never eaten sushi before so I thought that I would give it a go. I sat at the bar and ordered my meal and drink. My accent attracted some attention. I explained to the bartender my reason for being there rather than where most Brits went, that is to Florida! A local man who was sitting a couple of seats away asked if he could join me, as he was intrigued by the domes and had never met a real live Brit before! We chatted amiably and downed a couple of beers. He wished me a good evening and left. I finished off my beer and meal and called for the bill. The waitress said "Sir, your check has been taken care of"!

I never cease to be amazed or surprised by the kindness of strangers.

I duly completed my dome building course and returned home. I again contacted the Eco Dome charity but they had no opportunities for me. Frustration set in, so I resorted to the internet. I struck it lucky! A charity based in Walton-on-Thames was promoting Eco Dome habitations in various developing countries. After attending a series of meetings, the charity, in conjunction with an American church group, were prepared to send me to Zimbabwe!

The project was to build an orphanage for the child victims of the AIDS epidemic, which at the time was decimating the rural adult population of the township of Beatrice, about forty miles outside of the capital Harare. The dome habitation was to be constructed on a piece of land on a farm which had been formerly owned by a white family. The farm had been redistributed to a locally owned cooperative. I was ready for another adventure, but this one was to be somewhat different; no guns, no enemies. This time the tools of my trade would be a shovel and tamper tool. My motives were not monetary but humanitarian. I checked the Foreign and Commonwealth Office website for advice on travel to Zimbabwe. I was pleasantly surprised to see that unlike my previous destinations there was no banner headline screaming "Do not go there under any circumstances". Instead it merely advised caution, avoid political demonstrations and be aware after dark. So with my bags packed, off I flew to Harare. The charity funded my airfare and provided me with a small, daily per diem to cover my out-of-pocket expenses.

I was met at the airport by a local contact and conveyed to meet my new, Christian missionary friends, at the farm where the building was to be constructed. I had been forewarned that my accommodation would be basic, which I accepted - in fact it was my tent! I had brought with me a cheap solar shower, what more did I need? I was introduced to the farm labourers with whom I would be working. I pitched my tent alongside their huts in the worker's village and hung my solar shower from a nearby tree branch. I was shown the communal toilet facility, which consisted of a hole in the ground which was shielded by a wrap-around canvas cover. No paper was provided, as it was expected that each user would make their own provision for cleaning their nether regions! Next to the hole was a pile of ashes which was to be scooped up by hand and sprinkled down the hole to cover up one's deposit. Alongside the canvas-covered dry system latrine stood a plastic water butt for hand cleansing. I was to be fed by the local villagers in their communal dining area.

The next morning I was up bright and early. I had brought my own coffee with me. I headed over to the dining area where I scooped some close-to-boiling water from a large pot which was suspended over an open fire. I stood there sipping on my brew. The locals spoke an understandable form of English, along with their native Shona. As per my policy on all of my previous travels, I made a point of making friends with the locals. Some minutes later I was joined by my new Christian friends, who had just given thanks to the Lord for the new day. We got straight down to work discussing the plan for the building. All the materials and supplies were already on site. It was just a question of getting organised and getting going.

From my previous dealings in different developing countries, I was acutely aware that we should try and be sympathetic to local sensitivities and culture, rather than being the Western white men building them an alien-looking dome, whether they wanted one or not. I took note that the locals lived in circular "rondels" with thatched roofs. We collaborated with the villagers as to how we could build our dome to blend in with their rondel traditional habitations. Together we came up with a design which pleased the locals and satisfied my dome structure principles. The design was to be a central dome with a surrounding wall. A thatched roof would extend from the dome to the outer wall. The space between the dome wall and the outer wall was to be sectioned off, giving bedrooms for the orphans. The central dome area was for the house mother to live and for the children to relax in. The building would not be at odds with the rest of the village housing. The thatch would require replacing annually which gave employment to the village thatcher.

With agreement all round and our plan in place, we set about marking out the site and digging out the circular foundations. The following days were spent digging, ramming earth into the recycled plastic tubes, fitting the barbed wire, and coiling the tubes on top of each other. We tamped them down hard as they gradually corbelled inwards to form the hive shape, ready for the hand plastering of earth and cement, which was to be applied in a rough adobe style. The work was good honest labour, the local artisans quickly getting the knack of the build technique. The project was on target for the completion date. At the end of each day's work, as we gathered for dinner the villagers would entertain us by singing folk songs.

Those early evenings spent sipping cold beers, watching the sun going down, dinners cooked over an open fire, in a large round metal cauldron were quite magical. Our regular evening meal was a chicken stew which was unlike any chicken stew that I had ever eaten before! As we sat around the fire, one of the village women would stir the stew and ladle it out into our bowls, a claw or beak sometimes floating on the surface!

Everything was going well. My instinct told me that when things were going well then something would inevitably go wrong! Sure enough, one morning we were hard at work. The dome was up and work on the outer wall was about to commence, ready for the plastering and the thatched roof. I recall that it was midmorning, as I had just finished off my coffee, when three 4-wheel drive vehicles hove into sight. I leaned on my shovel and watched them approach, the other workers also stopped and stared as the dust cloud containing the vehicles grew bigger. The 4x4s drew to an abrupt halt and the dust cloud started to settle. Armed men in uniform spilled out of the trucks. Who the hell were they? Cops, military, bandits? Our locals were muttering in Shona. I could make out "Zanu, Zanu". One of our labourers whispered to me "Mugabe's goons, Zanu pf". The "goons" took up a circular position with their weapons pointing at us, which struck me as rather stupid because if they were to fire, they would surely have hit their own men. One of the elders of our artisans started addressing the "goons" in Shona. This went on for a minute or two. The voices raised and became more agitated. I was getting that same old sinking feeling again. My body was preparing for action. However unarmed and outnumbered, what could I do? I gripped my shovel. I started losing my patience with what now appeared to be a slanging match going on in front of me.

"Speak English", I shouted out.

The "goon" looked at me.

"I speak", he snarled.

I told him what we were doing.

He eyed me up and said, "You come to take back the farm?".

"No", I shouted, "what do you think this is?". I indicated the dome.

"Show me, white", he growled.

I then gave him a guided tour of our works. He seemed satisfied. When we returned outside, I suggested that to be sure of our intentions, why didn't he leave a guard here to watch us? The "goon" detailed three of his men to stand guard over us. He and his henchmen returned to their vehicles and stormed off. We resumed our work under the watchful gaze of our armed guards. After a while I felt uneasy, as the guards were fidgeting with their guns. The last thing that we needed was the danger of a negligent discharge of a weapon by a bored guard. I spoke to them. They were bored and agreed that they would rather be helping us doing physical work. Perfect, I had recruited three eager labourers! They laid their weapons down and got stuck into the task of digging and mixing earth and cement!

So the days passed; shortly after 0800 hours each day our guards would be dropped off, "to prevent us taking back the farm". They would take up their security positions and smoke cigarettes until their transport had disappeared from sight. They would then lay down their weapons and go to their labours with enthusiasm. Inevitably the day came when the final handful of mud and cement was slapped onto the dome and spread, adobe style. It was finished, job done! Such a feeling of satisfaction. The villagers gathered, food and drink was produced, the children sang and danced for us. Emotional goodbyes were sincerely expressed to the artisans and my American Christian friends. I was picked up by a local supporter and conveyed to Harare, where I spent the night before my morning flight back home. The next morning I was dropped off at the airport. I dined on a breakfast of coffee and a fried egg on toast. I can't remember the actual cost of the breakfast, but I do recall the piles of Zimbabwean dollars which covered the tabletop to pay the bill! At the time Zimbabwe was a victim of rampant inflation. I boarded the aeroplane, settled into my seat and felt good about myself.

Chapter 43
MV ADVANTAGE

It was a beautiful sunny, crisp, cold winter day. From the lounge window of my home I gazed at the sun rising over Royal Portbury docks. My bags were packed. The same old feelings of trepidation which I always felt before going on a job were there once more. No matter how many times I did this, the nerves were always there. I still haven't been able to make friends with them.

"I'm off to my class in a minute", says Frances, my long-suffering wife. She is my "rock", keeps me stable.

"I'll say goodbye now".

No nonsense, a hug, a kiss, an exchanged "Love you".

"See you in five weeks or so", she says as she disappears out of the door.

I watch her get into her VW Cabriolet, driving off with a wave and a blown kiss. I pick up one of our Birman cats. She senses that I'm off. I guess my bags in the hallway gave her a clue. Whilst cuddling her, my eyes rest on the hire car which the company provides me. The headlights and grille are like a face, and she was beckoning me. "Time to go", my internal voice orders me. I do my final checks, set the house alarm, grab my bags, slam the front door. The hire car is a Chevrolet. I'm not familiar with it so I chuck my bags on the back seat, settle into the driver's seat, get used to the knobs and switches and find BBC Radio 2. I fire the car up, whisper "Bye, home" and set off for Terminal 5 at Heathrow Airport. I had plenty of time so I drove steadily, no rush. Now that I was on my way, my nervousness gradually evaporated.

I stopped at Reading services for an all-day breakfast. So far my mobile phone has been silent, no messages from other team members. I knew Pat the team leader as I had worked with him on previous trips. He was a youngish former soldier who knew the score. The other two I did not know. In fact, one was on his maiden voyage as an anti-piracy operative. We made contact at a bar in Terminal 5, the start of our team-bonding process. The flight to Cairo was short compared to our usual destination of Colombo, Sri Lanka. Five hours later we met our agent, whose job it was to smooth our way through immigration and onto our onward minibus transport to Port Suez, where we were booked into the "delightful" Summer Palace hotel! I had stayed there a few times before, suffice to say it hadn't improved!

The next morning around 1000 hours our agent picks us up and we are conveyed to the port, where we negotiate officialdom more smoothly than usual. Could it be that our agent is a skilled negotiator, or maybe a little more generous than other agents? We found ourselves on the dockside where we sat on our bags, waiting for the launch to take us to the MV Advantage. Whilst we are sitting, generally watching the workings of the dock, a white van pulls up. Out jumps our agent who proceeds to open the rear doors of the van and lift out an off-white canvas hold-all, about four feet in length and one foot in girth. Judging by his awkwardness in handling it, the bag appeared to be weighty.

I looked at Pat, he looked at me. We didn't need telepathy to guess each other's thoughts, or what was in the hold-all.

I spoke first: "I was told this was a nice unarmed mission".

"Me too. I'm gonna ring the office now", said Pat, as he dialled his mobile phone.

He wandered off to make his call, returning a few minutes later.

"Crap communications as usual; we are not supplying weapons. These are the ship's guns and we can use them if we need them".

"I was told this was definitely an unarmed gig. We don't have helmets, body armour or tac vests", I complained.

As a group, we generally express our displeasure at being told one thing but finding the reality to be somewhat different. However we inevitably accept our fate, reasoning that since we are here, what else can we do? We are no longer in government service; private security is a different proposition, we are mercenaries so we get on with it.

We scramble aboard the launch designated to take us to our ship. After a choppy, 20 minute journey to the black-hulled MV Advantage, I was glad to get on board the stable deck which allowed my rising nausea to quickly subside. The chief mate greets us in a business-like manner, his accent is pure Bronx as he tells us to stow our kit away in our cabins and to join him in the "champagne room" in twenty minutes.

"Champagne room?" I exclaim.

"It's here on the main deck", he says.

Pedro, an *"AB" (able-bodied seaman)* shows us to our cabins. Mine was on the fourth stern poop deck, one down from the bridge. It was not the worst I've stayed in, equipped with bunk beds, en-suite toilet and a shower which would just about accommodate a dwarf! Bearing in mind that the ship was thirty odd years old, it came as no surprise to find the decor "tired". Pedro gave me directions to the optimistically-titled "champagne room". I dump my kit and go directly to the meeting room, which turned out to be totally devoid of champagne, or any other alcohol! The four of us sit and wait. General disparaging remarks about the state of our accommodation and the office communication failure feature strongly.

Normally the ship's captain greets us, giving us the "welcome aboard" pitch. However on this occasion Pete the chief mate gave us the greeting and advised us that Captain Valentio was busy right then, that we should get ourselves oriented and that he would see us at 0800 hours in the morning.

Pat said "Ok, what about the safety briefing, the weapons and 'hardening' the ship?".

"Tomorrow", was all that Pete said as he hurried off to his duties. We looked at each other quizzically. This was highly irregular. Usually the captain took charge, addressing us and asking questions in order to get a feel for us. Our TL would reel off our SOP's (Standard Operating Procedures). We would then set about "hardening" the ship with anti-piracy installations such as razor wire, as well as securing hatches and taking any other measures that we could to deter an attack.

The next morning straight after our excellent American breakfast in the galley, 0800 hours finds us once more in the champagne room. We are there greeted by a grizzly, heavily-set man who looked like a biker gang member, complete with long grey beard, wearing a red and white patterned bandana, with a grey pony tail hanging down to his shoulders. He wore an oil-stained faded blue denim work shirt underneath a black leather waistcoat, military camouflage combat trousers finishing off his look. I wondered if his Harley Davidson motorcycle was parked on the deck!

"Hi guys, I'm Hank, Chief Engineer. Captain Valentio has asked me to give you the guided tour."

He then gave us the official welcome brief and guided tour of the ship. He clearly loved his domain in the bowels of the ship, telling us that this had been his home since she was commissioned, "way back in '76".

"I guess you guys want to get on with pirate-proofing the ship?"

"What about us meeting the captain?" said Pat.

"He'll see you when you address the officers at 1600 hours" said Hank, as he turned and left us.

Pat, by now, was a little pissed off, as were we. Normal protocol was to meet the captain straight away, so that we could discuss and agree with him our graded response to any threat. "Let's just get on with the hardening" was our general consensus.

Pedro showed us to the ship's store, where we were issued with protective equipment and the coils of unruly razor wire, really nasty stuff which can deliver serious lacerations. Ship hardening is a tricky, dangerous job and it is impossible, even with protective kit, to handle the wire without sustaining at the very least minor puncture wounds! The job took us all morning. We stopped at 1130 hours, which is a universal maritime lunch break time. We continued until 1500 hours to finally complete fitting the wire to the ship's rails and any other vulnerable points. We also sealed headroom spaces with wooden pallets that we cut to fit individual apertures, then adorned them with the evil razor wire. The chief mate inspected our work and was pleased with our efforts. I went off for a quick workout, shower and afternoon tea, ready for our 1600 hour meeting with the captain.

Once more in the champagne room, the time 1600 hours. The ship's officers were there but no captain! We receive a communication that the captain would join us at 1700 hours. The officers drift off, saying "See ya later". Pat details me to sort out a medical kit and trauma pack. It seems that I was the only team member who had any relevant medical experience and actually held an in-date first aid qualification! Pat is seething and decides to go up to the bridge to confront the captain, as this situation was completely out of order. At 1645 hours I'm back in the "champagne room" with the "med" packs. Pat storms into the room.

"Lads I can only apologise, I have no idea what's going on. The captain has been in talks with the ship's owners and our lot. Our status is uncertain. Due to the threat levels this has to be an armed mission, however it was booked as unarmed hence we have no protective kit. It's questionable as to whether we are insured. I'm going to email the office to hopefully get some clarity in writing. So, let's just crack on as usual, get familiarised with our weapons and test fire 0800 hours tomorrow morning. At 0900 hours meet the crew and practice lockdown, then 1200 hours start our watches."

None of us are happy with being put into this situation. At 1800 hours we introduce ourselves to the ship's weaponry: two pump-action shotguns, a short-barrelled riot gun and a bolt-action sniper rifle. We acquaint ourselves with each gun. I had the most affinity with the Mossberg pump-action shotgun so claim it as my own. Whilst we were playing with our new toys, the captain and chief mate joined us, both carrying an ominous black canvas hold-all.

The captain gave us a short brief, and further told us that if there was going to be any shooting, that he and the chief mate didn't want to miss out on any of the fun! With that, the captain produced his own toy, a cowboy-era Winchester repeater lever-action rifle. The chief mate showed us his Remington shotgun. I looked at Pat and he shrugged his shoulders. What could we say? The captain has total control of all aspects of the safety and running of the ship. Once we were all satisfied with the workings of our guns we put them, together with boxes of cartridges, in our cabins and locked the doors. We agreed to meet Pat in the crew lounge after he had checked his emails for a response from the office. We grabbed some tea and sat in a huddle" chuntering" about our situation. Our job was the ship's security and dealing with any threats. The captain and crew's job was to sail the ship, ours was solely to protect it. On his return, Pat poured himself a coffee and said, "Nothing more than I expected from the office, basically we must play along with the captain to keep him sweet. Not even a 'Sorry for any misunderstanding".

So the situation is that if we have to stand to, the captain and chief mate will also be on deck with their guns, itching to "bag" a pirate! "If the shit goes down, they'd better stay out of our way" was the unanimous response.

Pat addressed us, "We are stuck in this situation, they are paying our wages, we have to play the game. Adjust, adapt and be flexible is the name of this game".

As I retreated to the ship's gym, intent on punching lumps out of the heavy bag, I silently reflected on where we found ourselves. This was totally extraordinary. Usually the ship's officers and crew were only too pleased to hand over the ship's security to us so that they could get on with the business of running the ship. This was light years away from the police or military operations that I had grown up with. We were steaming into the most dangerous waters in the world at the peak of piracy activity. Yes, the ship had speed but it had a low freeboard which meant that boarding would be easier. I knew that Pat was rock solid, that the other two guys would be good under pressure and that we would work as a team. The wild cards would be the "cowboys", in the shape of the captain and chief mate.

Pat had a word with the captain and chief mate, advising them that the protocol, should we come under attack, was for the whole crew including them to to go to the *citadel* (the safe room), from where the ship could be controlled and continue to be steered. Pat advised us that the captain's response was that it was his job to maintain the safety and integrity of the ship and that he would do everything in his power to ensure that. We went into a conclave speculating on various scenarios. We accepted that we couldn't force the captain off of the deck of his ship. Imagine advancing pirates, us trying to force the captain and chief mate into the citadel, they resist and point their guns at us! We rationalise that if things went really bad that it could be handy to have an extra two guns on deck. So, it was agreed that the captain and chief mate should be briefed on our tactics and act in support of us.

I felt much better after seriously "beasting" the punch bag and heaving some weights about. After all, I rationalised that on my last couple of jobs through the "corridor", that is the Internationally Recognised Transit Corridor (IRTC) through the Gulf of Aden, nothing much had happened. We had been averaging a speed of 15 knots per hour, with the capability to accelerate to maybe 20. No skiffs had probed us, no signs of "mother ships", from where the skiffs launched. In fact I had been on what were in effect paid cruises.

I had a shower and met the rest of the team in the galley. We talked it all through and decided to accept things the way they were. Basically, we were stuck with this situation! We agreed that should it come to it then the extra two guns must come under Pat's control in support of our tactics; however, there was some debate over who had authority to give the order to open fire. Ultimately it was the captain but he would have to come under Pat's authority in the application of our use of force.

At 0800 hours the next morning weapons were tested. We only fired two shots each to conserve ammunition. Len was designated sniper due to his military background. The third mate threw empty brown cardboard boxes over the stern for our practice shots. I reacted fast and was on target. The captain and chief mate blatted off a few rounds each. We were suitably impressed, just as long as they had the discipline. There was time for a coffee before we officially met the crew. Pat addressed them and, unusually for an American crew, they were very quiet. Some were old timers who had transited the Gulf of Aden, others were "GoA virgins". There were no questions at the end of the brief and it was back to work until 1020 hours when a practice drill would take place. At 1020 hours on the dot the buzzer roared out its continuous drone.

We ran to the bridge, drew our weapons and went to our stand to positions in all-round defence. The crew dutifully locked down in the citadel. The captain and chief mate remained on the bridge and relayed information to us regarding the simulated threat, which we reacted to in accordance with our tactics. They also practised the contact protocol for informing the relevant authorities and requesting assistance from the coalition protection vessels who patrolled the corridor. Satisfied with the drill, the captain called "endX" (end of exercise) at just before 1100 hours.

More coffee, lunch at 1130 hours then Pat and I commenced our sea watches at 1200 hours. By now we were entering the hot zone, "hot" in more ways than one! The sun was high and beating down. The Hanish Islands and Bab el-Mandeb strait, the "red hot zone" of the Gulf of Aden, where piracy was at its peak. Past the Port of Aden, then breaking out into the Indian Ocean 200 miles off the coast of Somalia, then turning west to Mombasa, Kenya, our next port of call.

And so began our routine of six hours on, six hours off. When nothing is happening, one piece of ocean looks extraordinarily like another piece of ocean. Even the slightest change of scenery causes great excitement. To see a pod of dolphins is enough for a tannoy announcement, which brings the entire crew on to the decks to watch them racing the ship. Such an uplifting sight! After four days of staring at the ocean we entered the Port of Aden at around 2000 hours. Cargo discharge immediately commenced. All cargo was unloaded and we were back out to sea by 0400 hours, heading off towards Mombasa. We settled back into our routine. The watches continued. Although only six hours long, they rotated around the clock and became tiring. No ships on the horizon, nothing on the radar, no reports coming over VHF10 radio. In my experience we should have seen or at least heard of something by then but no, not even a snippet of piracy intelligence from United Kingdom Maritime Trade Operations (UKMTO). This job was turning out to be quite unusual.

As far as we were concerned this was an unarmed deployment. Our standing operating procedures were that we would carry out our watches unarmed with the weapons locked away in a safe on the bridge. Off duty we would keep our guns in our cabins. Pat had a bit of a contretemps with the captain over this as he wanted us carrying loaded guns on watch. Pat stood his ground and the weapons remained locked away but available should we need them. Our joint experience was that a situation had never happened suddenly, and that we could go up the force continuum in stages which were contained in our Rules of Engagement, taken from the British Military Rules of Guidance.

I made the best use of my time on watch. Running around the deck using the ship's superstructure for body weight strength training pull ups and dips. I was still on watch and alert whilst keeping fit for my duties. The second mate who, judging by his physique, was obviously not into keeping fit suggested that I was a "slip, trip hazard", so I walked fast and wore a heavy backpack. The strength exercises I did away from general view kept me sharp and ready, rather than sitting down in the sun and feeling dozy!

The days passed, the nights passed. The moon was waxing and would be full by the tenth night out. I remembered from my police days that the volume of calls always increased when the moon was full. It was the tenth night out and the moon was as bright as it could be, there is no light pollution out there in the middle of the ocean. I had been in the crew lounge alone. It was 2330 hours and I had just finished watching the British classic movie, Get Carter. I poured myself a hot chocolate and retired to my cabin. I had to be up at 0530 hours ready for my 0600 hours watch. I settled into my bunk, sipping my hot chocolate. I was having difficulty keeping my eyes open. I checked the alarm on my phone. My hot choc was only half drunk when I drifted off into unconsciousness.

There was that noise again, that annoying buzzer sound. I open my eyes in the darkness and quickly remember where I am, in my bunk on board the US flagged ship MV Advantage. I'm part of an anti-piracy team. The noise has stopped. Must have dreamt it. If it was a real alarm it would be continuous. I reason "Well, something woke me!". I can't hear any other sounds. If it was the alarm then people would be shouting, doors banging, the sound of running feet. I heard nothing out of the ordinary. I check my watch and it reads 0150 hours. I had only been in bed for two hours. Pirates don't attack at night. Seeing as I'm awake, I figure I'll go for a pee. I squeeze into my cramped en-suite "head" (naval term for toilet). As I'm semi-consciously standing there urinating into the bowl, thinking I'll be back in my comfortable bed very shortly, my personal radio suddenly bursts into life.

"Third mate, are you doing headcount into the citadel?"

Realisation crashes my sleep-addled brain and I am instantly fully alert. Shit, lockdown, it was a genuine alarm. I swiftly slip into my uniform, grab my loaded Mossberg pump-action shotgun. In seconds, I'm down the stairs and onto the main deck, where I'm greeted with "Nice of you to join us", from Pat the team leader (TL).

"Is it a drill?" I ask, trying to mitigate my late arrival.

"Fuck no!" says the TL as he indicates a skiff off our stern starboard quarter and steadily gaining on us. The night is clear with a full moon. There can be no mistake. I can clearly see the skiff with figures on board.

I was up on deck and moving into a cover position on the port side of the bridge. This gave me a view of the stern, the rest of our tcam and the skiff that was cutting through the waves, clearly leaving a white wake behind it. It was running parallel to us and holding position, showing no navigation lights. Pat crouched down beside me.

"I didn't mean that back there, they sounded it in three bursts. It's only 'cos the captain hammered on my door that I got here", he said.

"It's ok mate, but I thought it was supposed to be a continuous blast?"

"Yeah, we'll address that one in the debrief."

The story he relates is that a large vessel has been sighted around fifteen miles off our port stern at midnight and remains there tracking us. It must be a mother ship, from which small skiffs can launch and carry out attacks. The skiff only appeared a few minutes ago. Radar failed to pick it up. There appear to be five crew on board. The captain has given permission to fire a warning shot. Len knows the score and won't fire unless it makes an aggressive move towards us. The second mate is calling UKMTO. That was it, watch and wait. "OK mate", was all I said as I settled into a comfortable shooting position. My senses ratcheted up. I was calm, accepting my fate: survive or die! Pat went to Len. We knew the drill, we had talked it through, walked it through, rehearsed it. Now it was the real thing. I had been in these situations a good few times before and the enemy had backed off, usually with a show of bravado by firing into the air as they retreated. Surely it would be the same this time! I could see the shapes of humans on the skiff, crouched low. Surely there was only one reason for them being there.

But hang on a minute! Pirates don't attack at night, or do they? I was aware that the only out-of-hours attacks recorded had been just after dusk, or just before dawn. All other attacks had been in the daytime in full sunlight, never in the dead of night. No, this was just a probe to test our reactions. They would maintain distance, follow us for a while then break off, return to their mother ship, rest up and maybe revisit us in the morning. The second mate would have sent messages out by now, but it would just be regarded as an intelligence report of interest, due to the fact that this was a nighttime probe. I was calm, pulse rate regular, alert and watching. However my mind was processing just how different from all of my previous transits this had been. An uneasy feeling crept over me. Instinctively I reached into the thigh pocket of my combat trousers and felt for my little yellow ships issue spongy ear protectors. I reasoned that it was obligatory "health and safety" to wear ear protection for practice shoots, so it wouldn't feel right if I hadn't inserted them in my ears in a real shoot situation.

The skiff had gradually closed, was about 150 metres and drawing parallel; they were poised and creeping closer. Contrary to popular belief they do not come racing in to attack at speed. My experience has always been that they would show no immediate signs of aggression, as this would give the intended victims notice of their intentions and the opportunity to make a preemptive strike. By slowly closing, they could monitor the ship's state of readiness. For them it was a game of subterfuge; one minute innocent fishermen, then once they had innocently slipped into range to attack, they became vicious pirates. In the past I have known them waving empty water bottles or sheets with "refugee" scrawled on in an attempt to appeal to our humanitarian instincts, so that we drop our guard and allow them to draw close to receive aid. It was then that the AK-47's would appear from under covers on the deck of the skiff.

Seconds seem like minutes. The skiff can be clearly seen in the light of the full moon. It's now trailing us in the bright, white luminescence of our wake. We can see the five members of the skiffs crew but none appear to be bearing arms. Pat gives the order for us to show weapons, in accordance with our use of force continuum rules of engagement. We take it in turns to quickly stand up with our weapons held aloft above our heads in both hands. We are exposed for probably less than two seconds each. It was at this point that I expected the skiff to either drop back or veer off back to the mother ship but no, it held its course. It was now about fifty metres away from us and doggedly closing. Pat has a brief conversation with the captain then his words come through my radio earpiece.

"Len, I've had enough of this, give him a warning shot."

I hear the distinctive "click, clicking" of the bolt action of Len's rifle as he chambers a round.

Len firmly says "Ready".

Pat commands "Fire!".

I see and hear the simultaneous crack and muzzle flash of the round on its trajectory into the sea, about ten metres in front of the skiff. Instantly the response from the skiff is a short burst of automatic gun fire. I was genuinely surprised, as this was totally unexpected. I recall saying out loud, "cheeky fuckers". Pat commanded us to hold our fire. My senses were super charged but I felt calm. I thought to myself, "ear plugs!". A pal of mine had sustained serious hearing damage due to exposure to unprotected shooting activities. I fished out my earplugs and deliberately inserted one in each ear, whilst maintaining my aim on the skiff. The wind and the engine noise were still there but now muffled. My training days on the range in Haiti drift through my mind. Mike intoning "Watch and shoot, watch and shoot".

More seconds masquerading as minutes pass by. The skiff is still there. Pat tells Len to try another shot closer to its bows. Len obliges: crack, flash, a spout of water erupts within feet of the skiff's bows. The skiff replies with another short burst. This time I flinch as I hear the whine of ricochet rounds rattling off of the ship's superstructure. Shit, this is getting dangerous; a stray ricochet is just as capable of killing you as an aimed shot. The skiff is now closing fast to get under the shelter of our overhanging stern. I wonder if these pirates are out of their heads after chewing khat? (narcotic herb). They could quickly be within grappling hook range and we would have to break cover, expose ourselves and go to the stern to engage them. We were at a critical point now, but we had the advantages of height, cover and a stable deck. I remember thinking "we cannot be taken". The skiff was a clear target, I had it in my sights, with five slug rounds in the breach and one in the chamber of my Mossberg pump-action shotgun. Our rules of engagement required us to only give one warning shot. Our discipline held. We had already given two.

Pat cried out for a third, "crack"!

The instant response was a fuselage of automatic gunfire from the skiff which was about to be lost from view.

Pat yelled the word "fire".

The next few seconds was a cacophony of noise and thumps to my right shoulder. Then silence, apart from the wind and engine thrum.

Pat shouts, "All ok?".

We all respond in the affirmative. I reload. There is no further automatic gun fire. Pat orders us to stay in cover and asks if anyone can see the skiff. No one can see it. The atmosphere is tense. Will we see and hear grappling hooks clattering onto the deck, thrown by the crew of the skiff? We remain in cover, scanning the stern and the wake beyond. Minutes pass, nothing. After fifteen minutes Pat gives the order for a tactical advance to the stern. We move deftly in sequence, weapons in the aim, covering each other in turn until we reach the stern. We scan the sea behind us, straining our eyes, but there's nothing, apart from the lights of the mother ship in the distance some miles away. In pairs we check along the port and starboard sides of the ship. We then return to the stern. We lower our weapons and gather for a hot debrief. Pat confirms to the captain that the threat is over but to maintain full speed ahead. The crew are released from the citadel. We adjourn to the crew lounge for a hot chocolate and an even hotter debrief!

After much debate we came up with three scenarios:

1. We sank it.

2. It was lost to sight under the stern overhang and made good its escape during the fifteen minutes that we waited before breaking cover.

3. Variations of 1 and 2. The captain joined us and reported that the mother ship had moved to the location of our contact with the skiff.

The remainder of this leg of our voyage was uneventful. We arrived in Mombasa a few days later. Late on the second morning the captain summoned us to the champagne room. Also present were two men in their late twenties, dressed in polo shirts and light-coloured chino trousers. They introduced themselves by job title only: "US Naval intelligence". The spokesman of the pair told us that they had read the captain's report and asked if we had anything to add. We were all aware of the content of the captain's report, as we had helped him to compile it. We gave a negative response. The spokesman told us that the attack had occurred in international waters and that our measured use of force was reasonable in the circumstances. Intelligence from land-based sources monitoring pirate activity reported no evidence of any such attack or loss of life. In that case, as far as we are concerned it never happened, he concluded.

"Have a good day, gentlemen", was his departing comment.

I guess it was all just a bad dream?

Preparing to Board MV Advantage

Chapter 44

THE TALE OF THE YEMENI CAT AND THE DISAPPEARING LUNCH

W e were on yet another American-flagged ship. I can't remember the name of it. However I do recall that we were to discharge our cargo in the port of Aden, Yemen. Before we entered the port, the captain addressed us and advised us that due to the civil war that was ripping the country apart, there would be no shore leave, under no circumstances must anyone wear any military-type clothing and that our weapons were to be hidden and locked away in the ship's safe. In fact, as far as the crew manifest was concerned we were described as "supernumeraries", work study consultants analysing working procedures. We were to perform our rotating security watches, but undercover, wearing civilian clothing, carrying clip boards and making out to any onlookers that we were intensely watching the ship's working practices.

I was the designated team leader. I passed this news onto my team. All accepted the situation apart from one, the new guy. This was his first deployment in private security. He insisted that his camouflage bush hat was not military and that everybody wore them! I knew that he was just being a twat, because he resented me being team leader. He had recently completed his twenty two years in the army. According to him I was just a "fucking plod and weekend warrior" (derogatory term for police and military reservists). The fact that I had 12 years of maritime security, most of it as a TL, didn't cut it with him.

It had got to the stage where he wanted to fight me to see who should be TL, however he appeared to be too busy to meet me in the ship's gym! It was to be his first watch and he had been firmly ordered not to wear his bush hat. He walked towards me to relieve me from duty with his bush hat perched on his head at a jaunty angle. Before he knew it, I had whipped it off and had thrown it over the side! I called his bluff. After an eyeball-to-eyeball stare out, he backed down.

I was on a morning shift, dutifully patrolling the deck and keenly observing the efforts of the stevedores. In the distance outside of the port gates, the flash and bangs of armoury could be distinctly seen and heard. I was casually leaning on the ship's rail, staring idly at the goings-on. On the dockside right in front of me, lying flat on its side was a huge rubber tractor tyre that had apparently been discarded there. The workers used it as an improvised seat during cigarette breaks. Whilst I was casually casting my gaze around the scene of dockside industry I noticed something moving at the edge of the tyre. No one was sitting on it, in fact no one was near it. I concentrated my attention on the tyre. It was a black furry head poking out from what must have been a hole in the tread of the tyre. It was the dock's resident cat! Kitty had set up home inside the redundant tyre. It took a look around then returned back inside its lair.

A few minutes later three young Yemeni stevedores take up position, sitting with their feet inside the centre of the tyre, oblivious to the presence of the furry creature beneath their backsides! They unwrap parcels and start tucking into their lunches. A fourth older man approaches the tyre, choosing to sit with his feet outside the edge of the tyre with his back to the other three. He also proceeds to unwrap his packed lunch. As he is doing this his mobile phone rings. In his haste to answer his phone he stands up and places his partly-unwrapped food on the floor. I guess it was an urgent phone call as he walks off gabbling away on his phone. As I watch this mundane scene of everyday dock life, I notice a black furry paw tentatively feeling around, quickly followed by a black furry head. I can only assume that puss has smelt the food. Puss boldly creeps forward, extending its right front paw, expertly hooks the food pack and quickly drags it back inside its rubbery home! The fourth man completes his phone call and returns to enjoy his lunch. The other three have been eating and chattering, blissfully unaware of the disappearing lunch! The fourth man looks on the ground but no trace of his meal! Obviously I can't understand a word that is being said but the body language and gestures could have come straight out of an old silent movie. Voices are raised and it becomes a scene of pure slapstick comedy, with the fourth man vigorously pointing at each of the three accusingly. The three are shoulder shrugging with open hands, shaking their heads in denial, vehemently denying all knowledge. Lots of shouting ensues. Arm waving follows with the fourth man slapping each of the three men about their heads and chasing them along the dockside! I have to grip the handrail as I'm in danger of falling over because I'm laughing so hard. I did wonder if the cheeky resourceful cat did this on a daily basis.

Chapter 45
TAMIL TIGERS BOMB COLUMBO

It was late February 2009. I had been regularly carrying out anti-piracy duties aboard ships of various sizes and cargo, mainly as team leader but other times as a team member. I wasn't bothered as either role suited me. Some guys would only accept jobs if they were TL. I had no ego, for me it was all about the adventure, but others sought the prestige and the extra money. The business was starting to get organised. From the unarmed, early days of throwing scrap metal or threatening attackers with burning petrol, we had become well armed with the Rules of Engagement and extremely effective. Up until now the only qualification required to work in anti-piracy was an "ENG1", which was a medical certificate that proved a minimum standard of health. Now there were floating armouries and a company had established an armoury in the departure port of Galle, Sri Lanka for the issue of weapons. The security industry in the UK had become legislated and licensed. The maritime security industry as a whole would no doubt follow.

The floating armouries stored weapons, ammunition and provided accommodation for teams between deployments. These boats stayed in international waters offshore, but in a relatively safe position before the entry to the International Transit Corridor. I recall one was an old cutter-type vessel where the onboard conditions were less than five-star cruise standard! The other was an ancient wooden barge with no inside sleeping accommodation. The only fresh water was bottled and strictly for drinking, not washing. However I spent many a pleasant night on a mat on deck, drifting off to sleep, gazing up at the amazing night sky which was enhanced by the lack of light pollution. Personal hygiene was a question of adapting to the environment! Shaving was accomplished by squirting foam onto your face then scraping it away with your razor. Once liquid soap had been liberally applied and massaged into your important bits, rinsing off was accomplished by simply jumping over the side into the sea, having first brushed your teeth so that you could wash your mouth out in the salty ocean!

After touching down in Columbo, Sri Lanka and being met by the agent, I was conveyed to a nice hotel. A team decision was made to visit the rhythm and blues bar that had been recommended to us and which was within walking distance. After dinner we set off to the bar. I remember that it was downstairs in a basement and that it was fairly busy. The three of us sat at the bar enjoying our Lion beers. It must have been around 2130 hours when suddenly the lights went out. Instinctively I grabbed my beer with my left hand and my right hand covered my wallet which was in the right rear pocket of my jeans, but no one tried to rob us! Was it a power cut? The music had also ceased. There was confusion, raised voices and a general movement of bodies towards the stairs to exit. We were on our feet and also moving to the stairs. We joined the throng, pushing our way upwards without spilling a drop of beer! We were part way up the stairs when I heard and felt a "whumpf" which caused the building to shake. This motivated me to escape from the building in short time. When I was outside everything was dark. No street lights, only car headlights. What was it, a bomb, an earthquake? The three of us stood there trying to orientate our way back to the hotel. With that we looked up to the sky and saw flashes of red fireworks.

"Shit, that's tracer!", I exclaimed.

This was confirmed by the thump of heavy artillery. A police car pulled up and an officer was talking to the gathering. We asked what was going on. Another officer approached us and told us in English that the Tamil Tigers had launched two airplanes and were on a bombing mission. One had been shot down and had crashed into a building close to our location. Ground forces had fired anti-aircraft missiles at the attacking planes and downed the other, which had crashed into a building in the next street. We could hear the sound of emergency vehicles attending the explosion. We managed to grab a taxi and get safely back to our hotel. The next morning the television news gave detailed reports of last night's attack. It was another close call for me. I started to wonder if I was pushing my luck.

Chapter 46
MOMBASA

M ombasa was one of my favourite ports, for no reason other than something always seemed to be going on there. I recall being on watch during discharge operations. I'd be leaning on the starboard rail, monitoring the local workforce and remaining alert to the possibility of stowaways secreting themselves in the most obscure of nooks or crannies. The most common and dangerous hidey-hole was the anchor chain locker. Standard practice was to mount a guard on it in the hours leading up to setting sail. Along with our anti-piracy operations at sea, our in-port responsibility was for the prevention and detection of stowaways. This duty was a very high priority, as once in international waters any stowaways that were found became the responsibility of the ship to treat them humanely. It is the duty of the shipping line to repatriate them, together with all the administration and aggravation involved, not to mention looking after their welfare and covering any costs entailed. The situation became much more complicated should the stowaway wish to claim asylum and seek refugee status!

Our cargo was mainly mixed foodstuffs that are commercial along with humanitarian aid. Thousands of the instantly-recognisable, donated UN World Food Programme, blue logo-bearing white sacks of rice were being off loaded onto trucks and driven off the dock, together with commercial goods. I couldn't help noticing that a stockpile of UN and commercial goods was building up along the side of one of the dock buildings. I also noticed that workers were blatantly taking items from this pile. A series of small pick-up trucks appeared, loaded up and drove off. My old copper's head told me that I was witnessing acts of blatant theft. The chief mate was on deck duty overseeing operations. I pointed out to him what was going on. He shrugged his shoulders and sarcastically explained the principle of "acceptable wastage".

"That pile, as you can clearly see, is damaged or spoiled goods. It's an accepted practice for the dock workers to benefit from it."

"OK, I accept that, but what about the pick-up trucks?"

"Ah, those will be the local traders collecting their produce to sell at the market."

He paused, then went on.

"We unload the cargo, then once it's on the dock side we have completed our part of the contract, what happens from there on is down to the recipients."

He further told me about the time a few years ago when a group of American farmers had donated some reconditioned John Deere agricultural machinery to farmers in Angola. Customs officers had boarded the ship at anchor off Freetown to inspect the delivery manifest. The captain had proudly informed the officers that the machinery was a gift from the farmers of America. The officials demanded 30,000USD import duty. The captain was at pains to explain that this was a "free gift". The officials were adamant that the tax was due. A flurry of phone calls to the intended recipients and donors came up with no resolution. So the tax was not paid and the machinery remained on board. The problem now facing the captain was that at his next port of call he was due to take on board cargo which was already paid for. Cargo loading is a strict science; weight, size and shapes had to be precisely worked out in advance in order that the ship was "trim", that is stable and safe to sail with the weight equally distributed. Enquiries at the next port were just as blunt: "Import tax must be paid". In frustration and desperation, the captain ordered the "gift" to be dumped over the side, into the sea!

It was another time and a different ship, but the same port of Mombasa. I was again leaning on the starboard rail watching the workings of the stevedores and casual labourers when a disturbance broke out. It happened suddenly with no obvious cause. One man appeared to be picked on by two or three others. The victim goes to the floor. I can't make out what the shouting is about but it's clear that one man is taking a beating as others start joining in raining fists down on him. Although it was nothing to do with me, I couldn't stand by and do nothing. Instinctively I'm running down the gangway. As I'm heading towards the fracas I mentally note that others were joining in on the assault. It also occurs to me that as I set foot on the dockside I'm in a foreign country and have left any authority that I did have behind me, back on board the ship! I'm committed. By now five or six men are laying into the victim who is defenceless on the floor. The attackers are intent on doing harm to their victim and not aware of me charging into them. I sent the assailants sprawling. It was like playing rugby again, I had dropped my shoulders and spread my arms as if driving into a loose maul. They were all skinny build so it was no feat of strength but momentum which allowed me to bowl them over. I was standing over the now bloodied semiconscious victim. I was yelling at the attackers to "fuck off" as I raised my fists in a fighting stance.

The attackers gather themselves to their feet and start towards me. I repeat a snarled "fuck off". Their advance falters. I'm well aware that work has now come to a halt and that there are at least another fifteen or so other workers forming up behind the attackers. Shit! The odds weren't looking good for me or the victim. I shout out "Why do you beat him?" At the same time my personal radio crackled into life.

"Security, you ok? Status report."

I guess it must have been the radio transmission that caused the attackers to hesitate.

I respond "Third mate, third mate, assistance dockside, medic required. Out".

The attackers are now standing in front of me about three metres away.

Again I yell at them, "Why do you beat him?".

There is a tense moment of silence before the tall skinny man at the front of the mob sucks his teeth, spits on the floor and growls, "He is Eritrea".

I say, "OK but why beat him?".

I was aware of the fast-approaching ship's crew in my peripheral vision.

"He is illegal, we don't want him."

The third mate who is also the ship's medic is now beside me two AB's are now checking the injured man. The heat had been taken out of the situation.

I say to the third mate "Can we take him to the sick bay?", as I indicate the injured man who is now on his feet being supported by the AB's.

"Not a good idea, if we take him on board they won't work", says the third.

"OK let's get him into the dock office to sort him out" I say, as we move towards the building.

As we approach, a man emerges from the interior and stands in the doorway preventing our entry. He tells us that he will not have an Eritrean in his building. What do we do now? The third calls the captain and advises him of the situation. It is agreed that the captain will contact the ship's agent to call an ambulance which will be paid for from company funds. We drag the Eritrean into some shade to make him as comfortable as we can and clean up his bloodied face. The attackers disperse. After about thirty minutes an ambulance arrives and takes the casualty away. We returned back on board the ship. Work has resumed as if nothing had happened.

Chapter 47
THE CAPTAIN'S BODYGUARD

One of the most fascinating jobs aboard ship was working as the captain's bodyguard. Why it fascinated me was the opportunity it gave to observe human behaviour. Whenever a ship entered a port and was secured in its berth, immigration officials together with customs and police officers would come aboard to visit the captain in his office to complete their paperwork. It had become customary for the captain to present these officials with modest gifts, as a gesture of goodwill. This custom had grown up over the years to help smooth the wrinkles in any paperwork. The gifts consisted of cartons of 200 cigarettes and bottles of whisky. Alcohol was accepted universally, even in countries where it was forbidden! Each official would be issued with the standard 200 cigarettes and a bottle of whisky. However human nature being what it is, people get greedy. The problem for the captain was if he didn't comply with requests for extra cigs and/or booze then a problem with his paperwork might be discovered. Time is money in the shipping industry and any delays have a knock-on effect, such as being late for the next berth and having to wait offshore incurring more costs. So an extra carton and bottle was a small trade off to get things done. The trouble was the officials knew it too, which was where I came in.

A number of the ports that we visited in East Africa were former French colonies. My Haitian Kreyol was generally more or less understood there, which made me the choice for captain's bodyguard for the officials' visits. Although English was the maritime language at sea, in port it was a different matter. I was only too happy to help. I would be detailed to meet the officials and escort them up to the captain's office on the bridge, show them in, then stand in the doorway watching and listening. If the captain felt pressured by the officials, he would signal me to come in and I would politely ask them to leave. The fact that I could do it in a language they understood seemed to work as I never once had a difficult situation in all the years of me doing it.

I recall an occasion when I was performing such a duty when the last awkward official had left and an "AB" was escorting him off the ship. The American captain looked at me and said "Chris, you're one miserable-looking mother fucker". I fixed him with one of my looks and said deadpan, "Sir, I was born with a miserable face but I'm happy inside". The captain burst out laughing! I didn't think it was that funny but he obviously did! It was early evening. The captain invited me in, sat me down, poured us both a whisky and thanked me. We knocked our shots back. He then said, "The chief's in charge now, another?", as he poured out a second drink.

Chapter 48

JAIL TIME IN ODESA, UKRAINE

Another duty that I was selected for was to escort the regional manager of the shipping line when he travelled through certain countries. This was generally a pleasant duty as it was not high risk bodyguarding but more like accompanying a mate on his travels. The company would do a risk assessment of the countries that he was due to pass through and if the decision was made and the company insurance insisted on it then it was often me that got the job. Due to the manager's status it meant hotel upgrades and occasional flight upgrades. It was January 2004 when I had just completed a trip. I was in Barcelona and about to fly home when I had a phone call from the company asking if I fancied "looking after Jack". I immediately agreed as he and I got on well and the job would be more like a couple of mates on tour.

My flights were rearranged and I was booked on a flight to Istanbul and booked into a local smart hotel, I can't remember which one. I do recall having an early night and a taxi turning up after breakfast with Jack on board. Off we set to Istanbul Ataturk Airport, our destination Odesa, Ukraine then onto the port of Illichivsk. We successfully negotiated Turkish security, customs and immigration, finally receiving our exit stamps in our passports and into departures to wait for our flight.

The flight was uneventful and we landed in Odesa International Airport in heavy snow. An announcement was made telling us to remain in our seats and have our passports available for inspection as immigration officials would be shortly boarding the plane. We sat and waited. We were seated towards the rear of the plane. It also occurred to us that we seemed to be the only Western passengers on board. The immigration officials entered from the front of the plane. They looked more like combat soldiers as they wore camouflage uniforms and carried automatic assault rifles and sidearms. They systematically went through each passenger, questioning them and examining their documents.

As they drew close I had a sense of unease. The official stood in the aisles, held out his hand and beckoned with his fingers. I was nearest and handed him my passport. He spent a good few minutes checking each page without saying a word. He then gestured for Jack to hand over his passport. Again some minutes minutely inspecting his. The official then called his mate. I looked at Jack, he looked at me. Nothing was said but I had that sinking feeling in my gut that something was about to go wrong.

The two immigration officers had a conversation. The second officer ordered us to stay. He then quickly looked at the next three rows of passengers' passports. Then returned to his mate and us. Before I started asking what the problem was, both officers drew their handguns and gave us the order to come forward. We instinctively raised our hands and shuffled out of our seats. I politely asked what's going on, but stoney silence was their reply.

We were put into an unmarked truck with two armed guards who handcuffed us. We were then conveyed to what I presumed was the arrivals hall and taken to separate cells, where I was searched. My watch and wallet were taken off me, the cuffs were removed and I was left alone. Some hours later an officer entered my cell and told me in English that we had been arrested for a visa violation. I started protesting. He further told me that a representative had been appointed to help me resolve my difficulty. I was left again to sit and wait. I was losing track of time.

Eventually I was taken from the cell to an office where sitting at a desk was a swarthy man wearing a purple-coloured shell suit and a cheap leather-look jacket, smoking a cheroot. He didn't introduce himself but told me that he had been paid €100 from my wallet to represent me. An armed guard was standing behind me, so I thought it best to not make too much fuss. My representative showed me my passport and pointed out that the exit stamp was partial, about a third of the circular stamp was missing! I pleaded that it wasn't my fault but was that of the Turkish official. He told me that I should have checked it. We then had a short argument. I realised very quickly that the odds were stacked against me and that I had no option but to play the game. So, I resigned myself to sitting there, answering his mundane questions: name, age, date of birth. Eventually after about an hour and him studiously recording my answers he told me that he was ready to put my case to the immigration board. I was returned to my cell to wait. More hours passed before I was taken from my cell to the customs hall.

I presumed that my representative must have played a blinder, as it looked like I was getting released, given that I could see our bags stacked on a desk. Jack appeared and we sullenly greeted each other. Jack said "Let's get out of here and I'll fill you in".

We both kept our mouths shut, got outside and took a taxi to the hotel Frapolli in Odesa where we were booked in.

We had spent nine hours in custody with no food or drink so we quickly ordered a meal. Jack's story was much the same as mine, plus the fact that he had to contact the head office for authority to withdraw 1,200USD cash on the company credit card to pay the 600USD we were each fined for our visa "violations"!

Chapter 49

MADAGASCAR

O ur ship had been diverted to Madagascar. We were on a tramp ship which meant that we had loaded cargo bound for one port but the cargo agents had found a better price for it in another port. This is something that we accepted when we agreed to go on a tramp ship contract. The shortest jobs were eight to 10 days but because of the flexibility the contract could last a month or more. For example, the ship could get diverted to a port for a better price for its cargo. Once it is being discharged then it is down to the agents to find another load to collect and deliver. This often meant hanging about in a port or remaining at sea awaiting a berth. The longest I did was six weeks. It was on one of these extended voyages which found me in the port of Toamasina in Madagascar for about 10 days. As there were no discharge operations taking place, our watches were "flag waving", that is just showing a presence. Still watchful but low risk. I struck lucky with day shifts, which meant I could take advantage of runs ashore.

One evening I took the local rickshaw taxi service into town. I told my cyclist to take me to a nice local bar. He dropped me off at La Teressa bar in Toamasina city. So commenced my nightly visits for the duration of my stay in the port. It was apparent that this was an expats' bar, judging by the number of white faces and variety of languages spoken. I appeared to be the only Brit there. The local language was Malagasy, however I could make myself understood with my Haitian Kreyol patois, as Madagascar was a former French colony. It must have been the evening of day eight or nine when I had eaten my meal and I was enjoying one of my favourite pastimes of people watching. I took particular notice of a couple of white men who had a certain look about them that I recognised.

The bar was packed, the music was a bit too loud and the hubbub of chatter made specific conversations difficult to make out. I noticed that they were knocking back spirits and getting more animated and louder as the drinks went down. I recognised the distinctive harsh Belfast accents. Were they former RUC (Royal Ulster Constabulary)? I was intrigued and it was time for another beer. I sidled up to the busy bar, next to the two Belfast boys. They were both in their 50's, with rugby player-type builds, cropped hair and hard faces. It was necessary for me to raise my voice to order a Three Horse beer (THB is the beer of Madagascar).

The nearest Belfast boy turned to me and said "Fuckin' Brit". Realisation crashed into my head; these were not *old* RUC men! I looked directly at him and paused to let my eyes bore into his for about five seconds. Then said in a firm, positive voice, "You got a problem with that?". I continued to stare at him. Was it my imagination but did the bar go quiet for those few tense seconds before he smiled and said in a soft voice:

"Fuck, you're all right. I'll get that."

He then told the barmaid to put it on their slate.

"Won't you be joining us?", he said.

"Can I refuse?" I replied.

"We'd prefer it if you didn't".

Immediately I realised that I was in the presence of former paramilitaries.

They led me to a table towards the rear of the bar. The occupants of the table got up as we approached and vacated their seats without question. We sat down. My new "friends" introduced themselves as Mick and Pat.

"Of course you are", I cynically replied, not identifying myself.

My mind is racing. I've got to brazen this out. We sat down. Pat raised his glass to propose a toast. This could be difficult, flashes through my mind. If he makes a republican toast how do I respond?

There is a pulse-raising few seconds pause before Pat proclaims, "To the money!".

What a relief!

I respond enthusiastically "To the money", and take a long swallow.

Fast thinking now, how to get out of this? Where were my escape routes?

I put the bottle down and said, "So, what you doing out here then?".

They told me that after the Good Friday agreement in 1998, being Republicans they had to leave home to find alternative legitimate employment where their skills would be appreciated.

They had found their way out here and were now running the security for the mining operations, besides developing business in other areas, hence the influence that they had in the bar.

It was my turn now. I told them about my anti-piracy job. They told me that they were now entrepreneurs and wondered at the possibility of making inroads into my industry. They knew that anti-piracy security was run by former UK military personnel. I told them that it was all covered.

Pat grinned at me and said "So, what were you then?". My mind was racing, was I setting myself up to be kidnapped? Fuck it, brazen it out!

"I was in the police and military reserves before working around the world as a private military contractor".

"Did you kill any of ours?", asked Pat.

I looked squarely at him and answered truthfully: "I did not".

That seemed to take the heat out of the situation as we went on to tell stories of where we had worked around dangerous places of the world. We enjoyed a few more rounds of drinks. We were getting on like old mates! As the evening drew to a close. Mick asked me if I would like to come and work for them in the mines. The money was really good but it was a permanent appointment so I had to decline. We got up to leave and shook hands.

"Bet you were shitting yourself earlier?"

"I was a bit concerned."

He then went on to say that out here we were all mercenaries and that no one cared about your background. It was all about the money. They walked off into the night. I got into a rickshaw and instructed the cycler to take me to the port. As the warm wind and the mildly alcoholic fugue sensation enveloped me, I reflected on the absurdity of the evening. Just a few years previous we were sworn enemies and would have happily killed each other.

Another place, another time and now we were mates!

Chapter 50

HOME FROM THE SEA

It was now 2012. I had been at sea almost continuously since 2007. These were the years in which piracy activity in the Indian Ocean had reached a peak, when piracy probes and attacks became a daily occurrence. The industry had become much more regulated. I was now a merchant seaman, a card-and-discharge-book-carrying, registered merchant seaman. To qualify for this title I had attended training courses in sea survival, first aid, fire fighting, ship security, port security and weaponry skills. The cost of all of this, along with the ENG1 medical certificate, came to over 3,000GBP. It was now a far cry from the early days of throwing scrap metal at our adversaries, like a bunch of hooligans! This, together with the ship's physical security of razor wire, booby traps and private military contractors for protection. These combined measures had made the pirates' task that much more difficult.

The number of incidents of piracy was starting to fall. However the pirates and the agents were now in cahoots; intelligence reports told us that the agents were in the pay of the pirates and would feed them information. For example, they would give them the names of the ships that had armed British security on board and tell them not to bother with them when there were easier pickings to be had elsewhere. The International Transit Corridor was now patrolled by coalition warships with additional air cover. The threat level was plummeting. Our SOP was that upon sight of any skiffs we would go to our stand to position and raise our weapons aloft above our heads in both hands. Invariably the skiffs would get the message and leave us alone. In fact the job was losing its edge. We'd spend hours staring at the Indian Ocean and it became very monotonous, one section of sea looking the same as another. The risk was much reduced and the pay was reduced accordingly. The only time we qualified for the high rate of pay was when we travelled through the IRTC. But a ship travelling at 18 knots per hour would be clear of it in 24 hours, therefore we were only paid for one day at the high rate.

It wasn't just the pay issues that became a problem. The money was tightening up all around. Travel expenses were reduced. Our hotel accommodation had changed from single rooms to doubles. This was a shame, as I used to enjoy my solitary nights in the Lady Hill hotel in Galle before boarding a ship the next day. The long-haul flights which originally excited me were becoming a trial. Could it be that I was becoming jaded with the lifestyle? My first grandson was due to be born in May 2012. I really wanted to be at home for the birth so I told my employers that I was not available. But the inevitable happened and a job came in.

"We are desperate, it's only eight days, you're a TL, you can be there and back in time for the birth".

I worked it out and figured that I could just do it, so I agreed. Two days later I was getting off a plane in Oman and I switched my phone on. Ping! A text message. I opened it and it was a photo of a newborn baby. My first grandson! The caption read "Hello grandad, 15 minutes old". I went to pieces inside. I have never felt such overwhelming emotion. The next week dragged on. Back home the first thing I did was to visit my grandson.

I never went back to sea.

Chapter 51

ORCHARD STREET

" " I'm 63, what am I doing?" I mentally ask myself as I slowly get dressed in my security uniform of black and yellow. My SIA licence (Security Industry Authority) is around my neck, suspended on a lanyard. A man is supposed to become more mellow with age? Unfortunately my fuse has got shorter, I don't tolerate drunken yobs like I used to. So why was I dressed and ready to work as a licensed door supervisor, note, no longer a "bouncer"! I guess it's because it's what I've always done. I knew nothing else and this old dog was not one for new tricks, so what else could I do? I pull on my leather motorcycle jacket 1940's American air force style, kiss my wife goodbye, leave the house, pull my helmet on, fire up my retro-styled motorbike and zoom off into the early evening. My destination is the O2 Academy, Bristol city centre. It was a Friday evening and I was to perform security duty at a band night, which always finished at 2200 hours. By the time that we kicked out the last punters at 2230 hours, we were finished and home by 2300 hours for cocoa and bedtime. These gigs were easy numbers, I even enjoyed some of the music! Compared to the hard-nosed bouncer type work that I had done up until only a few years ago, this was a pleasure. I roared off into the night, enjoying the ride.

Bike securely locked opposite the venue; I stride into the Academy. I'm greeted by the young team members. They are all respectful and reverential. The gig goes off without incident and everybody has a good time. I have absolutely no recollection as to who the bands were. When the event closes we "sweep" the venue, that is check all areas to ensure that all members of the public have left. The time is approaching 2230 hours. Most of the security staff will be staying on duty to work the Ramshackle nightclub which follows the gig and goes on till 0300 hours. I'm just about to clock off duty when the security supervisor approaches me.

"Do you fancy earning some extra cash?"

I knew what was coming.

"We are short staffed on Ramshackle. I'm desperate, you can have the public relations job out in Orchard Street, just being a visible presence to deter noise."

Why my resistance was so low, I have no idea. The words "Ok, yes I'll do it", are tripping off my tongue whilst at the same time my brain is saying "You idiot, no, no, no!".

I'm duly briefed and venture out onto the well-lit Orchard Street wearing a "hi viz" vest and equipped with a radio. Orchard Street is a residential area of big old Victorian houses, mainly subdivided into flats. The patrol was to appease residents who had complained of antisocial behaviour by club leavers wending their way to the city centre for the late night eateries and taxis home. The usual catalogue of complaints was noise, urinating and the occasional fight. I could cope with that and the £40 on top of the gig money would make the night more worthwhile.

I patrol up and down the street. All nice and quiet. My supervisor stresses that this is purely a public relations exercise and I have no legal powers. I knew exactly what powers I had from my police days; I had those of an ordinary citizen, the main one being the right to self-defence. A couple of female residents offered me a cup of tea, telling me that they were pleased to see me on the street. This took me straight back to my police days on the beat. As the night wore on so people left the Academy and made their way to the city centre. Virtually everyone greeted me pleasantly. This was going to be an easy number! Around 0200 hours a couple of lanky young men in their early 20's, one of whom was wearing a baseball cap, entered Orchard Street. They were being quite loud and stood in a house doorway where they were preparing roll up cigarettes. I walked over to them, displaying open hand gestures and saying, "Hey lads, keep it down, people are trying to sleep".

The response came from the baseball cap youth.

"Security, fuck off or I will fuck you up."

I stood there looking at him sneering at me. I instantly felt my fuse fizzing. I had to control myself and not be provoked. I got a grip of my larynx and managed to say as calmly as I could. "I'll pretend I didn't hear that. Please keep the noise down", in the vain hope that they would heed my advice. In order to hopefully prevent the situation escalating, I immediately turned and walked away.

I had only gone a matter of five or six paces when I heard the snarled words "I said I'm going to fuck you up".

My fuse blew! I turned and retraced my steps up to "baseball cap". My situation-diffusion techniques had blown, along with my fuse! My blood stream was flooded instantly with adrenaline, cortisol and any other chemicals that I required for "fight or flight" syndrome. I felt supercharged and flight was not an option. His eyes bored into mine; he was in striking range.

"Come on then, fuck me up", I growled.

His hands were in front of his chest working on his roll up. He released his finger grip of his half-made cigarette and let it fall to the floor. I recognised this as a classic preparatory act to intended violence. I registered his right eye tightening into a squint, the right side of his face tensing up, the right side of his top lip pulling back exposing his teeth, his right shoulder lifting as his right hand clenched into a fist. My experience and training told me that his brain was sending a message to his right hand to form a fist to punch me. This happened in less than a second. He was focussed on my face and that was no doubt where he would aim his first blow. My hands were at waist height. My reactions were quicker than his. My right-hand punch came from my feet up, twisting from my hips to drive my fist hard into his gut. I felt his body lift with the force of it. He folded, his mate went to react and he got one in the gut too!

"Baseball cap" had sunk to his knees, his mate was leaning back against a wall holding his stomach.

I'm screaming at them to get up and fight.

"Baseball cap" is calling me some rather unpleasant names in between bringing up some of the beer that he had consumed that night.

The bravado had gone out of them. I yelled at them to "fuck off", pushing them both up the street.

They are now both staggering, trying to run. I'm yelling and chasing them, kicking them both up their asses. I had lost it.

It was hard work running and kicking them both, so after about 50 metres I gave up.

I turned and walked back into Orchard Street breathing hard. As I regained my breath I looked up. I spotted the close circuit television cameras. It dawned on me that my exploits had been captured on film. I stood there expecting the police to arrive but they didn't.

I had learnt my lesson; I needed to ease out of the more robust type of security work. I really didn't want the pinnacle of my illustrious career to be a prison sentence!

Chapter 52

GLASTONBURY EVICTIONS OFFICERS

I have a long connection with the world-famous Glastonbury Festival. My first experience was way back in 1974, just three months after the Bristol Constabulary amalgamated with the Somerset and Bath Constabulary to form the Avon and Somerset Constabulary. This meant that I could now volunteer to be deployed outside of the Bristol city limits if I so wished.

When the request circulated for paid overtime at the Pilton Pop Festival, as it was then known, I jumped at it. The festival was in its infancy in those days. I remember that on completion of our 1000 hours till 1800 hours shift, a group of us decided to stay on and enjoy the ambiance. We locked our uniform shirts, boots and helmets in our police car in the police compound and ventured onto the site, barefoot and bare chested. We enjoyed the atmosphere and ate some food before heading home.

Unfortunately as the festival grew and evolved to become the "Glastonbury Festival of Contemporary Performing Arts", our duties became more formalised and much more serious. There was no opportunity to shed our uniform and mingle with the crowds. Even so, it was one of the deployments that I looked forward to each year, right up until I retired from the police in 1995. As June 1996 approached, I made enquiries about working security there. Fortunately for me, a local security company had one of the main internal contracts. I would annually make myself available each subsequent year for "Glasto", that is if I wasn't overseas.

Over the years, security became a huge issue at the festival. The eviction of transgressors against the conditions of entry code developed from security staff throwing offenders into their vans, driving them off site and dumping them in the middle of nowhere, having removed their footwear and thrown them away! A system had now been introduced where security staff would have to take potential evictees to an eviction centre, where the security would state their reasons for evicting the offender to a pair of eviction officers. The potential evictee would be given the opportunity to state his or her case for remaining on site. More or less a copy of a police custody suite.

Jerry, a former senior police officer friend of mine and I were selected as night shift eviction officers. We had worked together on security jobs and run training courses. We knew each other well. He had a huge capacity for calm, due to his long-term practice of Tai Chi. I, on the other hand, was close to burnout with confrontational work. He was aware of my short fuse and regularly counselled me to seek calm. It was the 2014 festival and yes, we did see Dolly Parton on the Pyramid Stage, across a sea of 150,000 people!

The eviction centre was monitored by closed-circuit video and relayed to the security control centre. The night shift evictions were running into the 100's and we were both getting frazzled, I more than him. We had a number of evictees with whom we had to get physical. Much to the amusement of the control room supervisors who were watching us on CCTV, but equally to the consternation of the security staff, trying to maintain control of the ever-growing queue of freshly-arrived potential evictees. In fact one of the security supervisors came into the eviction portacabin and addressed me, saying "Can you go a bit easier? You're upsetting them and making our job more difficult". I apologised and gave myself a talking to. My Orchard Street encounter was still raw from a few short weeks ago. I admit that I was close to the edge.

It was around 0300 hours when a particularly obnoxious drugged up/drunk 20-something male was brought before us. The detaining security guard related the circumstances of his detention to us then left. Jerry asked him what he had to say for himself. I was doing the scribing, attempting to write down his response on the official forms. He was abusive, entitled and sneered down at us and in particular at me, as I had to clarify some of his replies in order to correctly record what he said. He was an arrogant, haughty, "posh boy", with the accent to go with it. He kept poking and prodding. It was as if he had sensed exactly what would wind me up. I felt the chemical reaction in my body. He was hitting all of my nerve endings! Jerry knew it too. I looked at Jerry, he looked at me, was it telepathy or the imperceptible nod of permission? I deliberately took my glasses off and laid them on the desk. I was boiling inside, ready to explode. It took all of my effort to control my voice.

"You have breached the conditions to remain on site, so you will be evicted. Please go outside where security will escort you off site."

He stood up and said condescendingly, "I refuse to be spoken to by plebs such as you, I demand to see your superior. I demand legal representation".

That was it! I was out of my seat in front of him. He was

similar height to me but lighter build.

"Last chance", I growled, "go now or I will help you".

"You wouldn't dare", he laughed in my face.

I heard Jerry saying "Chris". But it was too late, he had already challenged me! I grabbed the front of the military-type olive-coloured jacket that he wore. I lifted him off his feet. His face was now inches from mine, the arrogant sneer had instantly been replaced by a wide-eyed look of fear, very satisfying. My fists were now under his chin as I gripped his jacket and carried him a couple of yards to the portacabin door. I heard Jerry calling "Chris, no!" as I kicked the door open and threw him down the three steps into the mud outside. He landed on his back with an audible "ouff".

I stood in the doorway. The rowdy queue waiting for our attention went quiet. The two female police officers who were in overall charge started giggling.

"Get rid of this one please", I calmly said to whoever cared to hear it.

I was calm, having released the tension that I had been suppressing. As I turned Jerry was there. He went to the open door and called the security to give us a few minutes before they sent the next one in.

"Are you ok?", he enquired.

"I am now", I replied.

I knew that I had overdone it. Jerry wasn't judgemental; he sat me down and explained to me that if "posh boy" makes a complaint to the police, what was he supposed to say? I had compromised him and all the other security staff that had witnessed it. I knew all that of course but even so I had failed to control myself. I had become a liability to myself and to anyone else that I was to work with. Realisation started to creep over me. Jerry left me and went outside. I sat there contemplating my stupidity. I had to rethink my future.

Jerry returned after about 10 minutes. He advised me that "posh boy" was contrite and sorry for his behaviour, that it was due to the alcohol. The police spoke to him but he didn't want to make a complaint. I was very lucky. There was a knock at the door. A security supervisor was there offering me a mug of tea. Jerry told me that he would continue to deal with the evictees and for me to just sit and say nothing. The next few clients were rather subdued. We finished the shift without further incident.

I didn't sleep very well that morning. We agreed that as it was the last night shift, I would just be a physical presence. It was also agreed with the security staff that the presenting officer would remain with us until the evictee was dealt with. The shift went by without a serious incident. I held back and only assisted with the difficult ones.

After sleeping, packing up and driving home, Jerry counselled me that I had a very narrow escape and that I really must get out of hard contact security. I told him that I was sorry to have put him in such an invidious position and that I had some thinking to do.

FINAL THOUGHTS

After Glastonbury I still wanted to work. I have first aid qualifications, so I signed up with a private ambulance company working on contract to the National Health Service in a support role covering shortfalls in patient transport services.

Projects that followed included:

Deployment overseas with a disaster management company to aircraft crash sites in Libya and France, recovering personal effects.

Working in London doing search and recovery operations at the Grenfell Tower fire.

Helping people with learning difficulties and/or challenging behaviour.

Seasonal work with the UK Border Force in France, England and Wales as an Immigration Officer.

Today I'm still very active including:

Working at professional sports events, providing medical cover to players and officials.

An instructor with a team-building company.

In my free time (chuckle), I spend time with my wife, children and grandchildren. I'm enjoying writing poetry and giving talks as a result of my two books being published.

NINE SIMPLE WORDS

"Never let your memories become greater than your dreams."

Nine simple words that have always guided me. They set me on a course that sent me far away on adventures to dangerous lands that would seriously test me.

And I'll conclude my book with my poem,

"Never Let Your Memories…"

I started off a copper seeing life in the raw

The worst of life, the best of life, all humanity was there

A lifetime dealing with people in distress left me battered, broken

and mentally bereft

Burnt out and beaten, it was time that I left

I had to leave, my neck was broke, the medics said to me.

"Go it's stable, live your life, you are free"

A regular job, a proper job, they all eluded me

Who'll employ a man with such an injury?

My skill set as a copper was violence in extreme

So I put my talents to good use in the world of security

CALL SIGN CHOPPER-THE SEQUEL

The pubs, the clubs, the fights, the fear, the camaraderie

The excitement, the adrenaline got its hook in me

Realisation dawned, I was pushing my luck

Tempted by the BBC I took a chance and went for it

But it was not to be, fame, fortune, celebrity!

Oh, what might have been?

Depressed, unsure, a fiftieth birthday facing me

"Never let your memories" re-inspired me

I packed my bags and off I went to the vodou land of Haiti

The thrills, the fears, the escapades cured my mental malaise

I had to be on my mettle just to stay alive

Iraq was next then Haiti once again

Things were kicking off at sea. I pit my wits and took a chance on anti-piracy

The boredom, the shootouts, the tension all got a grip of me

My first grandson born, impacted hard

I came back home aged all of sixty-three

I saw my boy and I made a vow to not go back to sea

My adventure years were over but what more could I do?

Security at festivals would hopefully see me through?

As a warrior grows older, more mellow should he be?

Unfortunately this progression did not apply to me

My fuse grew short, my temper flared, I became a liability

Now that I am seventy with a full life behind me

Chris Nott

CALL SIGN CHOPPER-THE SEQUEL

I often sit and ponder what I've done and where I've been

The mantra that ruled my life I recite inside my head

"Never let your memories" will inspire me till I'm dead.

Chris Nott
October 2020

To learn more about Chris's schedule and the possibility of him speaking at your event, contact his agent Christine Scrivens at:

chrissbookings@outlook.com

You can also visit his website at:

CallSignChopper.com

Chris Nott
Portishead, England
November 2023

Printed in Great Britain
by Amazon